Starting from Scratch

What You Should Know about Food and Cooking

Written by Sarah Elton
Illustrated by Jeff Kulak

For Abha, Anil, Amir, Anouk, Altair, Anisa, Avelene, Farah, Fiona, Hana, Kareem, Mayah, Meena, Mikyle, Mkhaya, Nadia, Nimah, Pema, Saskia, Sevan, Trudy, Uma, Zain, and every child who loves the taste of delicious food. —Sarah Elton

For Marku! Thank you for sharing so many amazing meals. —Jeff Kulak

---

Owlkids Books acknowledges the financial support of the Canada Council for the Arts, the Ontario Arts Council, the Government of Canada through the Canada Book Fund (CBF) and the Government of Ontario through the Ontario Media Development Corporation's Book Initiative for our publishing activities.

Published in Canada by
Owlkids Books Inc.
10 Lower Spadina Avenue
Toronto, ON M5V 2Z2

Published in the United States by
Owlkids Books Inc.
1700 Fourth Street
Berkeley, CA 94710

Library and Archives Canada Cataloguing in Publication

Elton, Sarah, 1975-, author
      Starting from scratch : what you should know about food
and cooking / written by Sarah Elton ; illustrated and designed by
Jeff Kulak.

Includes index.
ISBN 978-1-926973-96-8 (bound)

      1. Food--Juvenile literature. 2. Cooking--Juvenile literature.
I. Kulak, Jeff, 1983-, illustrator II. Title.

Library of Congress Control Number: 2013949442

Design: Jeff Kulak

Manufactured in Chai Wan, Hong Kong, in October 2013, by Printing Express Ltd.
Job #13-07-008

A   B   C   D   E   F

Publisher of Chirp, chickaDEE and OWL
www.owlkidsbooks.com

4 Introduction
Why Should You Cook?

6 Chapter One
What Would Life Taste Like Without Food?

20 Chapter Two
We Are What We Eat

32 Chapter Three
Cooking Is Science

44 Chapter Four
What Is a Recipe?

56 Chapter Five
Getting Ready in the Kitchen

68 Chapter Six
How to Make That Meal

88 Conclusion
So What Dish Will You Make?

96 Index

Introduction
Why Should You Cook?

It's easy to open a can of soup. Making macaroni and cheese from a box is a cinch. And you'll have dinner on the table in no time if you buy a frozen lasagna and heat it in the microwave.

But if you make that soup from scratch—or the mac and cheese, or the lasagna—it's a lot more work. So why should you make food from scratch? There are plenty of reasons to cook for yourself.

To start, cooking can be fun. Turning raw ingredients into a delicious meal is an art. It's like painting a picture or writing a story or composing a song. Once you get the hang of it, cooking becomes easier and easier—and the food you make will become tastier and tastier.

Food can be fascinating, too. There are all sorts of incredible things that happen to food when we prepare it. We can use chemical reactions to transition ingredients from one state to another, such as turning cream into ice cream. We even use little critters like bacteria and yeast to transform what nature has given us into the stuff we put in our mouths.

There's more! When you cook, you are figuring out how to look after yourself and the people you care about. Knowing how to cook makes you independent. It's part of growing up.

And cooking is bigger than simply making dinner. Preparing food is a kind of language. And that means that when you make a meal for people, you are communicating with them. You're telling them a story about who you are and what you like to eat.

In the end, when you cook something tasty, it not only makes people happy but also makes you feel good. It feels terrific to hear someone else say: "This is delicious!" And when you take a bite, you can enjoy the food, too.

Chapter One
What Would Life Taste Like Without Food?

We can't live without food. We eat to fuel our bodies. Food gives us the energy we need to learn, to play, to work, to think, to sing and jump and laugh and breathe.

And get this: what you eat becomes *you*. Really! Your body will turn the food you swallow into the building blocks for all the cells that make up you. When you eat, say, a sandwich, your digestive tract absorbs all the nutrients you need to be healthy and strong.

Food makes us who we are in other ways, too. Just think of the food traditions that are special to your family. Is there a birthday dish you look forward to eating? Does someone in your family make the same holiday treats every year? What about when you get sick?

To help a child get well, some parents will make congee—a rice porridge—while others will prepare a piping hot bowl of chicken soup.

But you could say that the most important thing about food is its taste. After all, whether or not you *like* what you put in your mouth comes down to the flavors *in* your mouth. Your other senses also help you decide how much you enjoy what you are eating. What the food looks like, how it feels in your mouth, and even the sounds of your meal all shape your appreciation. So how does this whole sensory experience work? What *is* going on in your mouth—and your brain—when you take a bite?

Let's find out!

The Building Blocks of Taste

Why does food taste so good? It really does. Just think of the burst of sweet watermelon juice in your mouth when you take a bite of the perfect slice. Imagine the crunch of a homemade cookie, fresh from the oven. The taste of yummy food makes you happy. So what is it that you're tasting in your mouth?

The tastes on your tongue

People have been thinking about how taste works for thousands of years. In ancient China, cooks believed that there were five tastes, each associated with the five elements:

- Water—Salty
- Earth—Sweet
- Fire—Bitter
- Wood—Sour
- Metal—Pungent

For a long time, people in the Western world believed that there were only four tastes. However, it turns out that the ancient Chinese were right: we humans can recognize five distinct tastes when we eat (as well as many aromas).

Salty This is an easy one. We are programmed to love the taste of salt. Can you taste it in your mouth right now? That's why we love potato chips, French fries, salted peanuts, and popcorn. Salt also enhances all other flavors. It will make your spaghetti sauce taste more spaghetti sauce-y. It will make your stew taste more stew-y. And—yes, it's true—a pinch will even make your dessert more dessert-y!

Sweet Yummmm, sweet. Sweet like icing on a cake. Sweet like ice cream. Sweet like marshmallows and candy and caramel sauce. Sugar made from the sugarcane plant is our number one source of sweet, but up until recently, this kind of sugar was really expensive. There are other sources of sweet, too. Sugar in fruit is called **fructose**—for most of human history, fruits were the sweet fix people longed for.

Bitter This is a sharp taste in the mouth. Coffee is so bitter it even *smells* bitter. Pure chocolate is also bitter. It can make your mouth pucker and feel dry. There are some foods we like even though they have this quality. One of the best examples is bitter melon. It looks like a cucumber with spikes and got its name for a good reason: its flesh tastes bitter, even when cooked.

Sour Sour is different from bitter. It's tart and sharp. Lemon juice is sour. So is vinegar. That's because sour is the taste of acid. We like to use the tartness of sour foods in our cooking, too. We also use tartness in drinks such as lemonade and in dishes such as salads. Chefs will tell you that sour notes from a squeeze of lemon or a dash of vinegar will make a dish "sing"—this means that it has a real zing to it!

Umami This is the new kid on the block. Umami was first identified in 1909 by a Japanese chemistry professor in Tokyo. But it took the rest of the world many decades to accept his finding. Umami is often described as a meaty flavor. It's that rich, round taste you get in your mouth when you eat foods like bacon or Parmesan cheese. The word "umami" comes from the Japanese *umai,* which means "delicious."

What's an aftertaste?

Have you ever eaten something that tasted really good at first but left a bad flavor in your mouth after you swallowed? The taste you feel right after you've eaten is called an **aftertaste**. Many cheeses are described as having an aftertaste. This isn't necessarily a bad thing. If you eat black licorice, a spice like cardamom, or herbs such as mint or basil, their flavor will linger in your mouth in a pleasant way.

Oooh, that's spicy!

When you eat something flavored with chili peppers, your mouth burns. Maybe your eyes even water! But spiciness isn't actually a flavor or a taste. It's a sensation. It makes your mouth feel a certain way. People who study and write about taste call it **piquancy.** You can make food spicy with all sorts of peppers—habanero peppers, Cajun peppers, black pepper, and more.

A tasty treasure hunt

Can you find the five building blocks of taste in your kitchen? You will likely find more salty and sweet foods than bitter or sour ones. That's because when we cook, we tend to use sour or bitter ingredients in smaller amounts—you don't need a lot of lemon juice to add zing to your dish. But you're going to need a lot of sugar to make those sweet cookies. And while you need only a pinch of salt to season your meal, salt is used in nearly everything we eat.

Which flavors do *you* like best?

Best (Taste) Buds

Go to the mirror and stick out your tongue. See a lot of little pink polka dots? Each of these is a spot—called a **taste papilla**—where many of your taste buds are clustered. The individual taste buds that help your brain interpret the flavors you put in your mouth are too small to see with the naked eye.

And taste buds are not just on your tongue. They're on the roof of your mouth (called your **soft palate**), at the back of your throat, and just about everywhere else in your mouth. Not long ago, people thought that different parts of your tongue were responsible for tasting different flavors. But research has proved that wrong. Now we know that all parts of your tongue can taste all flavors.

So why do we taste different flavors?
Flavors help keep us healthy and alive. Taste encourages us to eat, while different flavors encourage us to eat the variety of foods our body needs.

We humans are programmed to love the sweetness of sugar. Our body needs the energy found in foods such as grains and fruit in the form of **carbohydrates**.

All "carbs" are broken down by the body into sugars. Without these, our body doesn't work.

Salt stimulates our appetites. It's also important—in small amounts—for our body functions.

Meats provide us with protein and other nutrients.

Fats give food flavor and your body energy. They also give you all sorts of important nutrients that help your body do things, like make hormones.

Fruits and veggies give us lots of essential vitamins.

Because our taste buds tell us that we like to eat all sorts of flavors, we end up eating a variety of foods. The key to a healthy diet is not to eat too much of anything—except veggies. It's good to eat lots of different veggies.

Taste guard

Taste also protects our bodies. When something tastes bad, we don't eat it. That's good because poisonous things tend to be very bitter and sour. When our ancestors were hunter-gatherers—living off what they could collect in nature—they used their sense of taste to keep themselves from eating poisonous foods. When food goes "off"—starts to rot or mold—it also has a bad taste and sometimes even a bad smell. This signals us to stop eating something that could make us sick.

A bird? A plane?
No! It's a super taster!

Some of us love to eat the spiciest curries, while others faint at the thought of putting black pepper on our beans and rice. Why? It isn't necessarily just about what you prefer. The people who can eat more spice typically have fewer taste buds on their tongues! In fact, there are two kinds of tongues:

1 Super taster

2 Normal taster

If you were to look at a person's tongue under a microscope, you could count the number of taste buds. The super taster's tongue is wallpapered with them!

Super taster powers

Super tasters experience things differently than those without their powers. They often don't like drinks that have strong flavors, such as coffee. They also tend not to enjoy fatty foods, like spareribs or icing on cake, and they can't tolerate spicy or bitter foods. But that doesn't mean that super tasters don't enjoy their food. Researchers have found lots of super tasters in chef schools. These people love the flavors they taste and have highly sensitive palates. They use their superpowers for the forces of good-food-ness by cooking for the rest of us!

What's that taste?

Scientists discovered these super tasters by chance. One day, a researcher working in a lab accidentally released a chemical into the air. The other person in the room complained, saying how bad that chemical tasted. The first researcher didn't understand what all the fuss was about—he couldn't taste anything at all. With further research, he put people into two categories: the super tasters and the normal tasters.

What's in a Bite?

When you take a bite of a bright red apple, you taste the tart sweetness of the fruit. But you also hear a crunch, feel the juice in your mouth, and smell its perfume. What we call **flavor** is in fact a combination of what we smell, what we taste in our mouths, and what the food feels like. When we eat, we use all of our senses. Here's how each of our five senses works.

1 **Sight.** You use your eyes first to evaluate what you're going to eat. Just by looking, you know if you're going to eat a cookie or a banana. The color of your food also affects how you taste. In one experiment, scientists colored a red cherry drink with orange dye and gave it to people to try. Because the drink was an orange color, people thought they were sipping orange juice! Sight enhances our experience of flavor.

2 **Smell.** Smell is an important part of taste. You know just how important it is if you've ever eaten something you love when you have a cold. A stuffy nose will change the taste of what you put in your mouth—that favorite food likely won't taste as good. The smell of what you're about to eat, as well as what you smell as you eat it, helps you enjoy your food!

3 **Touch.** When you put food in your mouth, your nerves start to interpret the texture and the temperature of it. Your mouth tells you if a food is crispy or soft, crunchy or liquid, grainy or silken, hot or cold. This is what people in the food business call "mouthfeel"—it is literally what your mouth feels. Touch also helps you to know whether you like the food you're eating. You expect chewy gummy bears but not chewy chicken!

One smelly fruit

Some foods we love to eat also happen to smell bad. Fermented fish sauce—called *nuoc mam* in Vietnamese—smells funny to some but adds a scrumptious tang to all sorts of dishes. Many delicious French cheeses also have a strong odor. There's a good reason people call them stinky cheeses!

But possibly the smelliest food of all is the durian. This large, spiky green fruit smells so bad that in Singapore, it is against the law to eat one in public! Durian fans, however, rave about its fantastic flavor. If you haven't tried durian, you might want to start with a milkshake made with frozen chunks of the fruit. It's not so pungent when it's frosty!

4   **Hearing.** Even your ears help out when you eat. That crunch of an apple or the sound of hot tea being poured into your mug will shape your meal. Scientists have also looked at how other sounds—like music in a restaurant or the noise of an airplane engine—affect your eating experience. They report that the louder it is around you, the less you taste. Noise gets in the way of flavor!

5   **Taste.** To sum it up, taste is that unique quality a food has when you put it in your mouth—that "something" that makes one food different from everything else.

Food is flavor!

When your mind puts all these five senses together, you get flavor! Your brain combines the information from your five senses to tell you whether you like the food you're eating—or not! The strength of a flavor is like the volume of music. Is it a soft flavor, like a lullaby sung in a soothing voice? Or is it a loud one, like a car stereo blasting so strong that you can hear it down the road?

The no-smell challenge

If our noses help us to taste, can we taste without their help? Let's find out! See if you can taste the difference between an apple and an onion when your nose is plugged by a clothespin.

What you'll need:
- one slice of fresh apple
- one slice of fresh onion
- a grater
- a clothespin
- a helper

1   Grate the apple and onion separately. (Make sure you wash your grater in between.) Place the gratings beside each other on a plate.

2   Wash your hands with soap to clean away the onion smell.

3   Put the clothespin on your nose so you can't smell anything.

4   Close your eyes and ask your helper to put a spoonful of either the apple or the onion in your mouth. Ask her not to tell you which one she is feeding you!

5   Now taste the other food, too.

Conclusion
Chances are that because you can't smell what you're putting in your mouth, you'll find it hard to tell the difference between the apple and the onion.

Taste Is Tops

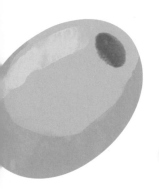

Are you salty or sweet?

If you were given the choice between a bag of potato chips or a piece of chocolate cake, what would you choose? Are you salty or are you sweet? Although we talk about people having a sweet tooth or a weakness for salty foods, in truth everyone craves different foods at different times.

Switcheroo

Scientists have shown that the food mothers eat when they are pregnant influences what babies like when they are born. But that doesn't mean our tastes are predetermined. As we get older, our tastes change. The foods that make you clamp your mouth shut now might be just what you look forward to eating one day. Hard to believe? Read on!

Acquired tastes There are foods you can grow to like—these are called acquired tastes. How many kids do you know who like coffee? Probably not many. Now think of how many adults can't start their day without a cup. Coffee and goat cheese are good examples of flavors that people say you need to get used to before you start to enjoy them.

Better at bitter Kids are more likely than adults to taste the bitter in foods. So as you grow up, you will become better at eating bitter foods. And you'll start to lose taste buds, too. The older you get, the fewer taste buds you have. If you don't like chili peppers now, that could mean that when you are eighty, you will be able to eat them raw!

Bad memories There are other reasons our tastes change. Let's say you get sick to your stomach after eating a lot of mushrooms. It could take you many years to start to like mushrooms again because the memory of feeling ill after eating them must fade first.

Growing out of taste?

Back in the 1950s, when products like canned soup and frozen dinners were becoming popular, people tried to imagine what food would be like in the future. (That's today!) Some people imagined that rather than eating dinner, we'd be feeding ourselves with pills. They predicted that science and technology would replace real food with food-like capsules. So you'd start your day with your breakfast pill. And instead of eating a bowl of spaghetti in the evening, you'd come home from school and take a dinner pill. No need to waste time tasting, chewing, and swallowing!

Were those people ever wrong! We still eat real food, not pills. Why would you want to skip the yummy taste of spaghetti? Or strawberries? Or cookies?

Taste in space

Taste is so important to our quality of life that scientists are trying to invent a way for astronauts to cook tasty food on their space missions. Today, astronauts eat a lot of dried foods, such as soup and cereal, which they rehydrate with hot water rather than cooking from scratch. They also eat things like granola bars, canned fruit, and premade casseroles in pouches. All this food must be prepared in zero gravity. (On Earth, gravity keeps the hot water in the pot.)

The problem with space food is that it doesn't taste as good as a home-cooked meal. Now NASA is planning to send astronauts to Mars in the 2030s—and that mission is expected to last more than two years! Mars has a little bit of gravity, which means the astronauts will be able to cook when they get there. This is important because eating real food makes us happy! If these astronauts are going to be away from Earth for so long, they'll need to find ways to connect with feelings of home. Tasty meals are the perfect way to do this.

FOOD FACT:
It's a miracle!

Some foods can change the taste of what you're eating. Did you know that artichokes make sweet flavors seem even sweeter? And miracle fruit is called just that because if you take a bite and then eat a lemon, it can turn a sour mouthful into something sugary sweet.

FOOD FACT:
No, thanks. I don't take sugar with my mouse!

Cats might like a sweet tummy rub, but they can't taste sweet when they eat. They are missing the genetic makeup that allows other mammals to taste sweet things.

The Wacky World of Flavor Science

Have you ever noticed that every carton of orange juice tastes exactly the same? Or that every box of a particular cereal is identical in texture and flavor? Or maybe you're curious to know why bubble gum tastes like bubble gum—does the flavor come from the gum tree?

This is the world of flavor science—a place where a food product's flavor is created by scientists. Flavor science gives **processed foods** their taste. Processed foods are store-bought products that have been made in a factory. They include products like breakfast cereals, granola bars, yogurt, salad dressing, and even orange juice.

But why?
When they make a processed food, scientists have to make sure that it doesn't spoil before you buy it at the supermarket and take it home. Often, they want to make the food last for months—or even years. This means doing two things. First, they have to heat it until all the harmful bacteria are killed (this process is called **pasteurization**— see Food Fact, page 34), and then they have to package the product with chemicals that delay spoiling (called **preservatives**). The problem is that after food goes through these processes, it doesn't taste good anymore. Enter the flavorist!

The taste lab
The people who create the tastes and aromas in the food products we buy at the store are called certified flavor chemists, or **flavorists**. These scientists have studied food chemistry and know a lot about the things that give all food a taste—their essential oils, their aromas, and their botanical (plant-based) extracts and essences. The job of the flavorist is to make sure that the food products we buy taste good. Every time. They do this by adding both natural and artificial flavors.

How are artificial flavors different from natural flavors?
Natural flavors are the aroma chemicals extracted from real foods and plants— like the oil in an orange peel. Artificial flavors are people's attempt to copy the flavors that nature created using chemicals from other sources. Scientists use lab equipment to figure out the molecular structures of the natural aroma chemicals in various foods and plants. So when a flavorist wants to build, say, an artificial orange flavor, she first determines what the aroma chemicals are in an orange. She then uses this knowledge to create a synthetic flavor chemical similar to the one found in a real orange.

This doesn't necessarily mean that scientists use raspberries to make natural raspberry flavor, or vanilla to make natural vanilla flavor. As long as the source of the flavor comes from nature, it is natural. **Castoreum** is a natural food additive used to flavor ice creams and sodas. It's natural, all right: it comes from a beaver's glands!

Why is there artificial color in my yogurt?

Flavors aren't the only things added to processed foods. Sometimes colors are added, too. That's because the natural colors of foods can be dull. And when food is processed, it tends to lose even more color. But people like to eat food that looks good and appetizing. That's why you'll see artificial color listed in the ingredients of many foods that you buy at the store.

Is it okay to eat these things?

Just because something is called a chemical, that doesn't mean it's bad for you. Your body relies on chemicals to work. Nature even makes them! (Humans make synthetic chemicals.) So just because flavor scientists use chemicals, that doesn't mean they are doing something scary. Then again, not all chemicals are good to eat (see BPA, page 61).

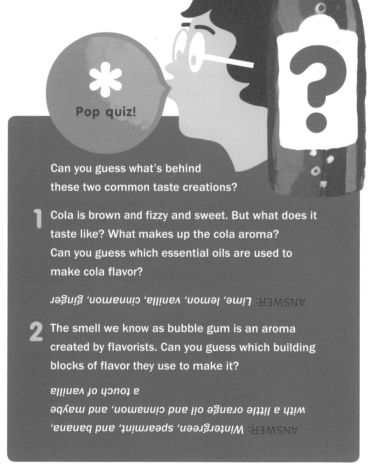

 EXPERT ADVICE: She's a flavor creator

Susie Bautista has been a flavorist for more than twenty years. She has a laboratory with lots of little bottles full of the captured aromas of all sorts of ingredients. When she needs to build a flavor, she first researches that aroma to find out what nature uses to make it. Then she'll take a little bit of this and a little bit of that, add a dash of something else, and...voilà! With the aromas in her little bottles, she can create the taste of a freshly baked apple pie or the creamiest vanilla ice cream. "It is a piece of art," says Susie. And just as each artist paints a distinct canvas, each flavorist creates something unique. Sometimes when she tastes another flavorist's work, Susie thinks, "It's amazing! How did they ever do that?"

Pop quiz!

Can you guess what's behind these two common taste creations?

1 Cola is brown and fizzy and sweet. But what does it taste like? What makes up the cola aroma? Can you guess which essential oils are used to make cola flavor?

ANSWER: Lime, lemon, vanilla, cinnamon, ginger

2 The smell we know as bubble gum is an aroma created by flavorists. Can you guess which building blocks of flavor they use to make it?

ANSWER: Wintergreen, spearmint, and banana, with a little orange oil and cinnamon, and maybe a touch of vanilla

What We Taste
When We Put Food in Our Mouths

We know that when we eat, we taste salty, sweet, umami, bitter, and sour. We can also sense a whole range of aromas. But when we eat some foods, we can perceive something more. That something is called **terroir**.

Terroir is a French word that describes the way that growing conditions affect the taste of food. The term was originally used by winemakers, but today we also use it for many different foods, including olive oil, chocolate, cheese—and even meats, such as chicken or lamb, and vegetables, such as carrots. All these foods have *terroir* because the taste of the final product is shaped by the place where it is grown.

The way this works is pretty neat. The oil made from olives grown on a really sunny farm in an Italian valley will taste different from the oil made from olives grown in Greece. That's because the soil is different, as is the climate and the amount of rainfall. All these factors will affect the way the olives grow and so will shape their flavor.

The **terroir** of cheese

Cheesemakers will often tell you that the secret behind their delicious product is its *terroir*. Get ready for a possibly mind-bending fact: the grasses animals eat affect the way their cheese tastes, looks, and even smells! For instance, in the summer months, when cows are out on the pasture eating fresh grass and flowers, the cheese made from their milk is more yellow in color and has a grassier flavor. In the winter months, when cows eat hay (which is dried grass), the cheese from their milk is paler and has a different flavor.

Their jobs are all about taste

There are people whose job it is to taste differences like these. You could say they get to eat for a living, but that wouldn't be the whole story. People who are knowledgeable about flavors have studied a lot to prepare themselves for their work. People who work with taste include the following:

Chocolatier

A chocolate expert who creates all sorts of concoctions by combining cacao with other flavors. Chocolatiers can work for big companies that buy millions of pounds of cacao beans or run their own shops.

Degustateur

(or *Maître Fromager*) A cheese taster who also sells cheese to the public. Degustateurs can also help cheese producers craft their recipes to make their cheeses better.

Sommelier

A person who works with wines. Sommeliers share their expertise with restaurants and vineyards.

All of these experts have learned a lot not only about food but also about how we experience what we eat.

EXPERT ADVICE:
Becoming a better taster

Julia Rogers is a taste educator whose specialty is cheese. If you offered her a piece, she might say: "In this cheese, you can taste brown butter and nuts." Or: "This cheese smells of ripe cream and melted butter, with just a hint of white mushrooms and earth." She uses a special vocabulary to describe the foods she eats. And you can, too. Julia believes kids are the perfect taste education students. "Kids are especially good at this because they don't have any preconceptions about what food tastes like," she says. "Kids don't hesitate to say it smells like crushed rocks or it smells like poo!"

How to begin

If you wanted to become a better pianist, you'd practice a lot. The same goes for tasting. When you eat something, try to find the right word to describe the sensation in your mouth. Pay attention to the flavor and then try to describe it. Later, try to remember what it tasted like. Take note of other smells around you. Julia says that people who work with taste are interested in the smells the rest of us don't pay much attention to. "What is the smell of the grass after a rain? What is the smell of the earth when it is dry? What is the smell of that wet spot in the basement?" she says. Try using these smells to describe the foods you eat.

Julia's taste experiment

Why not have an apple-tasting party? Choose three different kinds of apples—maybe a Granny Smith, a Pink Lady, and a Macintosh. Get a group of friends together and ask everyone to smell and then taste each piece of apple. Then have them rank their favorites and jot down their impressions. What do they smell? What do they taste? What's the texture like? Ask them to compare the smell of each sample and then the texture and the taste. Once everyone has written down their impressions, it's time to talk! Can your friends agree which apple is the best?

Chapter Two
We Are What We Eat

You've been eating since you were a small baby—longer than you've been able to talk or walk! You didn't know it, but when you were trying your first bites of solid food, you were being taught how to eat. What your parents chose to feed you not only filled your stomach but also introduced you to a particular food culture, or **cuisine**.

Not all babies around the world eat the same foods. Usually, the first solid food that babies in North America are served is rice cereal. This is a powder that comes in a box from the supermarket. You mix it with water or breast milk so it becomes a soft, easy-to-swallow dish, sometimes called **pabulum**. It looks nothing like grown-up food because it is designed specifically for babies.

But in some European countries, such as France and Italy, babies are traditionally fed foods that look more like what adults eat. Soon after they start eating solids, French babies taste leeks and green beans. In Italy, babies are given *brodo vegetale,* which is a strained vegetable broth.

In India, babies are first introduced to food by being given lentils, rice, and a grain called millet—they are often given bolder flavors, too, right from the start. And in other parts of Asia, babies are fed everything from rice porridge to mashed tofu to pumpkin.

In this way, babies' palates are shaped by the foods they are introduced to when they're young. And this continues as they grow into toddlers and then kids. Everywhere on Earth, people eat different foods in different ways. Many factors—from weather to local crops to traditions—help to shape people's tastes.

Even though food traditions everywhere are changing quickly because of globalization, cooking still says a lot about who you are and where you come from. What you choose to make when you start to cook—and how you choose to make it—reflects your identity.

You really are what you eat!

What Makes Different Cuisines Different?

Different countries have different styles of food. You could say that Italian cooking often involves pasta. Or that sushi is a Japanese meal. The distinct ways in which people of a certain place cook is called a cuisine. But the cuisine is shaped not only by the country people come from but also by what part of that country they're from—their region.

For example, pizza comes from Naples, a city in southern Italy, so it is originally a Neapolitan dish. Another famous Italian dish is risotto—a savory rice porridge. Risotto was more often prepared in the north, where rice grows, so we say it's typical of northern Italian cuisine. Each corner of Italy traditionally has had its own special dishes that make use of the ingredients available in that place.

Crops, climate, caravans, and creativity

These are the four biggest factors that have influenced regional cuisines.

Crops (and animals)

Over the centuries, people made their dinner with whatever foods grew best in their area. Maybe they lived in the mountains, where they could herd sheep or grow rice easily. Perhaps their crops thrived in a fertile river valley. Or maybe they lived by a sea, close to lots of fish.

Climate

Climate is the normal weather of an area. It affects not only the types of crops that can grow but also the types of food people like to eat. Think of which meals you prefer to eat on a chilly winter day rather than on a hot summer one.

Why is Mexican food spicier than French food?

For years, people thought that the hottest countries on Earth had the spiciest food. But no one had ever tested this idea. So a scientist named Paul Sherman at Cornell University in New York state decided to find out if this was correct. He and a research partner studied dozens of cookbooks from different countries. They looked at how many spices the recipes called for. They also noted how far that country was from the equator. They concluded that it was true: the closer you get to the equator, the spicier the food becomes.

But why? It turns out that spices like cloves and cayenne don't just make the food tasty, they help us out, too. Bacteria and viruses that can make you sick thrive in hot climates. Spices like turmeric stop bacteria from growing in the warm temperatures and help keep people from getting sick from organisms in their food! Over the course of history, people who cooked spicy foods were probably healthier. Their children would have been healthier, too. They would have learned to cook with the same spicy ingredients, passing this healthy habit to their own kids.

Caravans

Hundreds of years ago, merchants followed trade routes and shipped foods like spices over great distances in caravans and sailing ships. New foods came into towns and villages on these trade routes, introducing flavors and ingredients from one area into the cuisine of another.

Creativity

The first person to take a little bit of this and a little bit of that to concoct something delicious used creativity. It's easy to imagine that all recipes were started by a cook asking, "What if I do X?" This kind of imagination, daring, and invention has shaped the cuisines of the world.

Map Out Your Tastes

Chicken is a common food around the world. The bird was first raised in Asia thousands of years ago, but now it's eaten in San Francisco and Paris as well as in Beijing. People on every continent cook chicken for dinner. But that doesn't mean every chicken dish tastes the same. The way the meat is prepared and flavored reflects the place the meal comes from and the people who make it. The different ways we cook chicken show us the amazing variety in the cuisines of the world.

Canada

Roasted chicken with potatoes and carrots is a Canadian classic. There are many breeds of chickens, and the Chantecler breed comes from Quebec. It can withstand very cold winter weather and is tasty when roasted.

United States

Debate rages about how best to cook **southern-style fried chicken**. The chicken pieces are usually deep-fried in batter and are often eaten with potato salad and always with the fingers.

Mexico

Sopa de lima is a Mexican chicken soup flavored by sour limes. Typically, the clear, tangy chicken broth is topped with fried tortilla strips.

Venezuela

A popular Venezuelan food is **arepa**, a soft flatbread made from corn that can be stuffed. A national favorite is the **Reina Pepiada**, or the Curvy Queen—named after a 1950s beauty queen—that's filled with avocado, chicken, and mayo.

Morocco

Chicken tagine is a saucy stew that often features vegetables and tasty additions such as olives and nuts. It is cooked in an earthenware dish with a pointed lid.

France

People consider **coq au vin**—slow-cooked chicken with mushrooms, bacon, and red wine—to be a fancy dish today. But the dish's roots are in simple country cooking, which uses ingredients you have on hand.

Greece

Chicken souvlaki is a skewer of grilled breast meat often served with a flavorful sauce. Souvlaki appeals to an almost universal love for barbecued meat!

Lebanon

Shawarma joints sell sandwiches made from grilled chicken topped with garlic sauce, pickles, and very often French fries! It's tasty street fare that you can eat on the go.

Russia

To make **chicken Kiev,** you must pound flat a chicken breast, cover it in breadcrumbs, and then roll it around a pat of flavored butter. After it is baked and you cut into the meat, butter spurts out.

Kenya & Tanzania

When adventurers traveled the world, they introduced their flavors to the places they visited. **Kuku paka** is a saucy coconut chicken curry that blends the tastes of East Africa with those brought by Indian traders.

India & Pakistan

Chicken biryani is a dish made by layering meat and vegetables and a special spice mix, or masala, with rice. Different regions have different styles of making the dish, but it's always spicy and typically eaten with your hands.

Thailand

Massaman curry is a saucy, savory, spicy dish usually made with peanuts, fish sauce, and a tart fruit called tamarind. Its spices—star anise and cinnamon—were brought to Thailand by traders long ago.

China

In Szechuan province, street vendors make **bang-bang chicken.** In China, meat is typically cut into bite-sized pieces before cooking so it can be easily eaten with chopsticks. Bang-bang chicken got its name from the noise made when pounding the meat.

Japan

Chicken katsu is breaded and deep-fried, often seasoned with soy sauce and ginger, and served with rice. This is a casual meal.

You Say Tomato, I Say Columbus

What is more English than fish and chips? Or more Italian than tomato sauce? Or more Swiss than chocolate? These would be considered "authentic" foods. But it might surprise you to learn that a lot of the foods we consider to be authentic to a cuisine are in fact the new kids on the culinary block. If we look at the history of food, we can see that traditions never stand still. Cuisine is always changing.

Will travel for food!

Way back in the year 1491, no one in Europe had ever eaten a tomato. Europeans had never heard of corn. And they wouldn't have recognized a potato if you cut it up, fried it, and called it a French fry. Then, in 1492, Christopher Columbus sailed across the Atlantic Ocean and landed in what Europeans called the New World. Over the next few decades, explorers brought back potatoes, corn, and tomatoes—foods that had long been grown by the indigenous peoples who lived in the Americas.

In turn, the people living in the Americas were introduced to the foods that the Europeans brought over. They ate chicken for the first time, as well as crops like wheat and barley, which had been grown for thousands of years in the Middle East. This was the world's biggest exchange of food, and it changed cuisines all around the world.

The scary tomato

When the New World foods were brought back to Europe, a lot of people were scared of these strange new things. But soon enough, the Italians started using tomatoes to make the sauces they would one day become famous for. Someone in either France or Belgium (no one can agree exactly where) first cut potatoes into fingers and fried them crisp. And other New World foods, such as squash and turkey and chocolate, were enjoyed in places far from where they came from.

Restaurant fusion

Today, there aren't any new countries for explorers to discover. But as we try new foods and incorporate other people's recipes into our day-to-day lives, cooking still changes. In the 1970s, chefs in Europe invented a new style of cooking that built on this idea of exploring flavors from faraway. Chefs in France began to play around with recipes from Asia. They blended these flavors with their traditional dishes and created a new way of cooking. This mix-and-match approach was called **fusion**, and it quickly spread to restaurants around the world, where it's still popular today.

I'm game for a change

Meanwhile in North America, the foods of the indigenous peoples—like maple syrup and game meats (meaning the meat of wild animals), such as bear and wapiti (elk)—were used by the new settlers. In fact, the Europeans who traveled here would have died had they not learned from the people whose land they'd arrived in. An old cookbook from Quebec features a recipe for a salad dressed with bear oil—a perfect example of the blending of two food cultures.

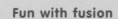

Fun with fusion

Can you do some fusion of your own? Dream up a menu for a meal that blends all sorts of different foods. How creative can you get?

Foods That Work

Many of the dishes we like to eat today were invented by people looking for ways to use the ingredients that were readily available to them at different times of the year. Other dishes were invented because they tasted good and would sweeten a special occasion—or even because they showed off a person's wealth. But some of the world's best-loved dishes were created out of necessity.

The super portable sammy!
Take the sandwich, for example. History tells us that the common sandwich—that's two pieces of bread with some filling wedged in between—was invented by John Montagu, 4th Earl of Sandwich, way back in the eighteenth century. He didn't want to leave the gambling table to eat his dinner (other people say it was his desk that he didn't want to get up from), so he asked his servants to serve him a meal in the form of two pieces of bread *sandwiching* a filling! A food with function was invented.

Good thinking

There are many other examples of smartly designed dishes.

Cholent   A stew made from meat, beans, barley, and vegetables, cholent is a traditional Jewish dish cooked overnight as you sleep—which helps religious families follow a Jewish law that says you can't cook on the Sabbath. If you cook cholent overnight, your dish will be ready for you to eat on the day when you aren't allowed to make it!

Labskaus   This is a German stew once popular with sailors working the seas in northern Europe. It was usually made with fish and hardy vegetables such as beets and potatoes that carried well— meaning they wouldn't go rotten—on long voyages. It is similar to a dish that people in England eat called scouse, which was also made with ingredients that could be found onboard—though scouse adds a dry biscuit to the recipe.

The kathi roll   This tasty snack is a roll-up sandwich that was invented in the Indian city of Kolkata in the 1930s. There are many stories that try to explain why someone decided to roll up some meat in a flatbread. Some say that the kathi roll was created for busy commuters to grab on the go. Others

believe the dish allowed the city's colonial British residents to eat kebabs without getting their fingers greasy. Whatever the reason, it's an easy food to eat with your hands—even while walking, if you so wish.

Pommes boulangère   A slow-cooked French dish of sliced potatoes and cream, this dish took advantage of the heat left over in a village oven after the baker had finished baking the bread. People could bring their pots of potatoes and cook them slowly, without burning any extra wood. They saved their resources this way!

The Lancashire hotpot   Invented during the 1800s, when more and more people in Great Britain were leaving the countryside to work long days in factories and mines, this one-pot meal of onions and lamb or mutton, covered with sliced potatoes, was assembled in the morning. It would sit in a warm oven all day so that dinner would be ready after a hard day's work. Panackelty is a similar slow-cooked meat-and-potatoes casserole from a different part of the country.

It's a Small World Indeed!

Many regions around the world have their own cuisines. And those cuisines can influence one another, especially since people move around a lot more today than they did even a hundred years ago. This means that cooking everywhere is changing. It's also changing because global businesses are moving foods around the world faster and farther than ever before. Every day, food travels long distances to reach our table.

On the move

Throughout history, we humans have always traveled with the foods we love to eat—or at least the seeds we needed to grow them. And as we traveled the world, we became better and better at transporting what we wanted to eat. Today, many of the fruits, vegetables, and meats that we eat travel from one end of the planet to the other—by plane, boat, train, and truck! Food doesn't stand still.

What's a season?

Modern transportation has changed the way we eat. For example, your great-grandparents would have had to wait until summer to enjoy ripe raspberries when they were in season. Those berries were considered a real treat! Now we can buy them—and whatever else we want—any day of the year. Even during the coldest months of winter, you can go to the supermarket and buy fresh raspberries. That's because they have been flown in from the southern hemisphere—the other side of the Earth—where it is summertime during our winter.

The world's supermarket

There are big companies whose business it is to move all this food around the world. And the same big companies that sell food in North America do business in other countries, too. You can go to a supermarket somewhere else and find many of the same foods from home—and you'll find the same fast-food restaurants, too. Because of this, people's food habits are changing faster than they ever have before. An organization called Oxfam asked people in seventeen different countries what foods they liked best. Are you surprised to learn the top choices were pizza and pasta?

The world's cuisine

The more that people choose spaghetti for dinner over dishes from their local cuisine, the more our tastes will become similar. If what we eat makes us who we are, this will mean that people around the world will become more and more the same. Some people are saddened by this trend. They believe the world is a richer place when there is more variety. What do you think?

Eat local, think global

Many people worry that shipping all this food around the world is bad for the environment. They believe that it's better to support family farmers who grow food sustainably in their local area rather than investing all the energy and resources needed to grow food on big, faraway farms and ship it to the supermarket. These people are sometimes called **locavores** (a word that was invented recently). They are part of a global social movement that is trying to make sustainable farming more common. For more information on sustainable foods, see page 67.

Chapter Three
Cooking Is Science

Cooking a meal is a beautiful thing. It connects us to our past, it tells a story, and it fills our stomachs. And the food we cook can be delicious. But when it comes down to it, what are we doing when we cook?

We're conducting science! Yep, science. When we heat up our ingredients, we are causing chemical and physical reactions in them. Quite simply, we're transforming matter from one state to another.

That makes *you* the scientist. And the kitchen? It's your laboratory.

A really good scrambled egg can taste like magic, especially if it is cooked just right, with some salt and maybe with a slice of buttered toast on the side. But the transformation you see as the egg changes from a liquid to a solid in your pan is not magic. It's science. That's because when you heat up the egg, you are changing its molecular structure. The egg white in your scramble turns from clear to white because its molecules are changing the way they connect.

So why not eat your food raw? After all, there are people who prefer a raw food diet. But cooking your food does more than change its molecular structure—it also makes the food taste good. And there's a bonus: cooking your food makes it less likely that you'll get sick from a food-borne illness.

But cooking food is about a lot more than just adding heat. Cold temperatures, salt, sugar, acids—all are tools we use to make our food last longer and taste better! This chapter introduces some of the chemical reactions and physical transformations that take place in our kitchens. It's science that you can eat!

Heat

Heat causes our food to change in texture, color, and taste. Compare the soft and tender flesh of a fresh, ripe tomato to the smooth, liquid texture of cooked tomato sauce. Depending on the chemical makeup of your raw ingredients, your food will change in a variety of ways when you add heat.

Meat + Heat

Meat is made up of things like water, proteins, and fat. **Protein** is a substance that your body needs in order to grow and stay healthy. When you cook meat, the proteins change. You can tell this is happening because the meat shrinks.

Veggies + Heat

Vegetables are mostly made of carbohydrates. But not all vegetables cook in the same way. Have you noticed that leafy greens like spinach don't look as bright after they're heated? That's because cooking affects the cells that turn plants green— these cells are called **chloroplasts**. When you heat up the spinach, the chloroplasts burst and the color becomes dull.

When you cook a potato, something else happens. Potatoes have starches. When you heat these up, the starch absorbs moisture and swells, and the cells burst. Potatoes are crunchy when they are raw because their cell walls are rigid. When these cell walls break as they are cooked, the potato becomes soft.

When you cook a vegetable like an onion, you transform the sugar within, making it sweeter.

Cooking kills the bad stuff

When you cook your food thoroughly, you are also killing many pesky little bugs, such as bacteria and molds that can make you sick.

FOOD FACT:
Heat kills bugs dead

In the olden days, people didn't know about bacteria. This was a big problem, particularly with milk. In the 1800s— when cities were growing and fewer people lived on farms—milk was shipped daily on trains and horse-pulled carts without ever being cooled. The bacteria in the milk had lots of chance to grow. Many got sick; some even died. A French scientist named Louis Pasteur, determined to fix this problem, created a method of boiling the milk to kill the bacteria. This is called **pasteurization**, after Louis himself.

Cold

Cold is used to preserve our food or to change its taste.

Freezing a food turns the water inside your peaches—or tomatoes or milk or meat—into ice. This stops the growth of the bacteria, molds, and fungi that can make us sick. The cold puts these little guys into a dormant, or sleeping, state. (Once you defrost that food, though, they'll start moving again.) That's why most foods last so long when they are kept at, or below, a constant 32°F (0°C)—aka frozen. They also retain their color, flavor, and nutritional content.

Not every food freezes well

The freezer is not for everything, though. Cooked egg whites become rubbery in the freezer, and potatoes take on a strange mealy texture. Fruit and vegetables also change when you put them in the freezer—when the water in their cells turns to ice, it breaks the cell walls, making the fruit or vegetable lose its shape and go soft when it thaws. This doesn't make the foods any less tasty—it just means you must find a different way to use them.

Cold treats

We also freeze things to create delicious treats like ice cream and popsicles. When we cool sweetened cream or fruit juice, ice crystals form. You must churn ice cream as it freezes to make sure no large crystals form and also to introduce air bubbles into the mix so you end up with creamy—not crunchy—ice cream!

Cool treats

For some foods, you don't have to drop the temperature below zero to change its state—chilling something in the fridge can work, too. Chill Jell-O and the liquid will set into a jiggling goo. Jell-O contains **gelatin**, which comes from a protein called **collagen**. When gelatin is heated and mixed with water, its protein molecules—they look like long pieces of string—begin wiggling around a lot. If you chill the mixture, these proteins stop wiggling and connect to each other, trapping the water in a matrix, or web, of cells that becomes your jiggling treat!

FOOD FACT:
What's freezer burn?

This isn't really a burn. When your food has freezer burn, it has lost its moisture. This causes it to change color and sometimes even texture. Freezer-burned food does not taste good.

Salt

We all need salt to survive. Our bodies won't work without it. But salt does a lot for us in the kitchen, too.

Cooks take advantage of salt's chemical properties. We use it to flavor foods because it enhances their taste. But it's also a good preservative—it stops meats, for instance, from rotting. Salt is also used for curing meats like ham, prosciutto, and bacon.

Salt draws water out...

If you put salt on a piece of meat, the salt draws out the water. By drawing out the water, the salt preserves the meat (called **curing**), because without water, it's harder for bacteria, yeast, and molds to grow.

...and salt draws water in!

A **brine** is water mixed with a lot of salt; it can be used to make meat more tender and juicy. The meat is soaked in the brine for several hours, and the salt helps the meat retain water in its cells. This means when it is cooked, the meat is moist.

Salt of the Earth, salt of the sea

There are two main types of salt: **rock salt**, which is mined from inside the Earth, and **sea salt**, which is harvested from evaporated seawater. We can also process rock salt and sea salt to create many additional kinds of salts.

Table salt   Table salt is rock salt that is processed into a fine crystal and treated with a chemical that keeps it from caking together. Salt makers have added iodine to table salt for almost one hundred years because our bodies need this element to be healthy.

Sea salts   These salts are also known as *fleur de sel*, gray salt, pink Peruvian salt, Hawaiian red sea salt, Maldon salt, and more. All these salts originate in the sea, but they're distinct from one another because of where they come from and how they are handled.

Kosher salt   Chefs like to use kosher salt, a salt with large crystals, because it is inexpensive and people say it has a clean taste. Kosher salt is the kind of salt traditionally used in a Jewish butcher shop to preserve meat.

Sweet

Most sugar is extracted from either the sugarcane plant or the sugar beet. This sugar used to be rare and expensive—kings and queens once showed off their riches with huge works of art made of sugar!

Today, sugar is cheap and plentiful. And like salt, it comes in many varieties— including icing sugar or golden demerara sugar. Not only do we use sugar to sweeten our foods, but we also use it for food preservation because it can stop the growth of microbes—like salt, sugar draws water from the cells of, say, a fruit, keeping it safer from nasty food bugs.

Sugar science
When sugar is heated, the molecules inside change and steam is released. If you cook sugar a little bit, you end up with a brown-colored caramel syrup. You can make hard candy by cooking sugar until it forms crystals.

Other sources of sweet
We love the taste of sweetness so much we've figured out lots of ways to have it!

Honey   We've been eating honey for thousands of years. Long ago, we would have collected it from wild beehives (there are still indigenous peoples who gather wild honey), but today, most honey is farmed.

Maple syrup   First Nations peoples in North America have long made maple syrup from the sap of the sugar maple tree. The sap, which runs in the spring, looks like water and has only a faint sugary taste. But if you boil it for many hours, it becomes the thick brown liquid we love to pour over pancakes.

High-fructose corn syrup Though you can't go to the store and buy a jar of this stuff, many of us eat high-fructose corn syrup every day. It is a sugar made by the food industry and used in many products, including soda pop and breakfast cereal.

Jaggery   This golden-colored sugar has a deep taste that is a bit like caramel. You make jaggery by boiling the sap from a palm tree or the juice from a sugarcane plant.

Palm sugar   In Southeast Asian countries, such as Burma and Thailand, people make this sugar from the palm tree.

Fat

Fats, such as butter and oil, give food flavor. We use fats to make delicious things. We rub butter into the skin of a chicken to help it turn brown when we are roasting the meat. We mix oil with vinegar to make salad dressing. We whip the fat in cream into a delicious mousse.

A world of fat

People use all sorts of fats when they cook: butter, olive oil, canola oil, coconut oil, ghee, and so much more. We also use animal fats such as lard (pig fat) and schmaltz (from the word for chicken fat in Yiddish).

Fat in action

Fats play many roles in cooking.

- We use oil in our frying pans to make sure food doesn't stick.
- We use fat to transfer heat to the ingredients we want to cook. When we deep-fry potatoes to make French fries, for example, we submerge the chopped potato in hot oil. This cooks the potato by surrounding it with heat carried by the fat.
- We use fat to make a rich, smooth icing for a cake. That's because many fats—like the butter in buttercream icing—are soft and smooth at room temperature.
- The fat molecules in cream can be used to trap air bubbles to make a mousse. That's what we call whipped cream.
- We use fat to make a cake. The fat in the batter traps the air and helps the cake to rise.
- When making pastry, the fat acts differently. We rub the fat into the flour. This is so that the fat surrounds the flour particles and keeps the flour from getting wet, and that means our pastry will be light and flaky.

Acid

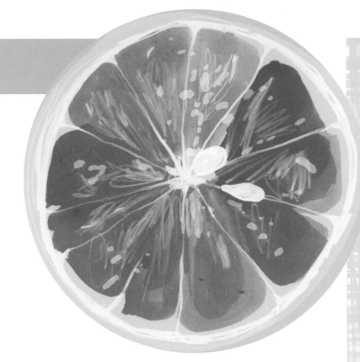

In the kitchen, an acid is a liquid like lemon juice or vinegar—something that has a sharp, sour taste.

A little acid can have a big impact on the flavor of your cooking. You can smuggle a bit into soups and stews and curries. You can even put some in sweet dishes like fruit sauces. The secret magic of an acid is that it makes flavors pop. It makes all the other ingredients say, "Hello! Taste me!"

Get dressed

Probably the most common place we use acid is in salad dressing. A salad dressing is what's called an oil-in-water **emulsion**. Boy, that's a mouthful! But it's really just a mixture of two liquids that don't naturally combine. The ingredients are whisked—or mixed very quickly—until they are blended. Mayonnaise is another tasty emulsion that you can find in a kitchen. You can make mayo yourself by blending oil and egg yolks with lemon juice or vinegar.

Look, Ma, no heat!

One amazing trick you can do with an acid such as lemon or lime juice is to use it to "cook" fish and seafood—without using any heat at all! In a dish called ceviche, the juice is added to pieces of raw fish, changing the protein structure of the fish's delicate flesh in a way that makes it appear to be cooked. But it isn't cooked, only **marinated** (meaning soaked in a flavorful liquid).

Acids also play an important role in preserving food because they stop microbes from growing and reproducing. We use acids to "pickle" foods such as onions and cucumbers. In fact, pickled cucumbers are the food we simply call pickles. For more on preserves, see page 42.

Bugs

We humans might do a lot of work in the kitchen, but we also ask our friends from nature to help out.

Some bacteria, fungi, and molds are bad for us, but there are lots that are helpful, too! We use bacteria to make things like yogurt, sour cream, sauerkraut, and cheese. Bacteria actually feed on the sugars in the raw ingredients in these foods and, in some cases, turn them into acids. This process is called **fermentation**. Yogurt is fermented milk; so is cottage cheese. Sour cream is fermented cream. Sauerkraut is fermented cabbage. All these are fermented by a few different kinds of lactic acid bacteria. We also use fungi and molds to make foods such as bread.

Sourdough, start your engines!

Sourdough is a bread that uses both bacteria and yeast to rise. People love it because it has a pleasant tangy flavor. To make sourdough, you use something called sourdough starter. That's a mix of water and flour that has collected bacteria and yeasts from the environment and fermented. People keep sourdough starter for years and years. It's kind of like a pet! As long as they keep feeding the creatures inside, the starter keeps growing and they can make loaf after loaf after loaf.

Hello, I'm Lactococcus lactis

Then there's cheese. When we make Cheddar cheese from milk, we use a bacterium called *Lactococcus lactis*. This bacterium ferments the natural sugars in the milk, creating **lactic acid**. Working with an enzyme called rennet, this acid curdles the milk—that is, it separates the milk solids, called the **curd**, from the watery part of the milk, the **whey**. We pour off the whey and then press the curd into a shape to make the cheese! Without these bacteria, none of this could happen. And while the cheese is ripening, the bacteria keep on working to help bring out the flavors in the cheese. *Penicillium* (the same one used to fight infections) makes blue cheese blue. And different sorts of *Penicillium* are used to ripen cheeses like Camembert or Brie.

And I'm yeast, a fungus

Yeast is another living thing that helps us to make yummy foods, especially bread. Technically, a yeast is a single-cell fungus. It eats sugar or starch and releases carbon dioxide—the gas that makes your soda pop fizzy. We use carbon dioxide to make bread dough puff up. To start making bread with store-bought yeast, you **proof** the yeast by putting its granules into warm water and feeding them a little sugar. This mixture will foam up before you add it to your dough. When you bake with yeast, you trap these gas bubbles in the gluten to make your dough rise.

Kneading

Kneading is done by pressing the heels of your hands into a dough and then folding it over. Then you do it again. And again. And again.

Make some dough

Take some flour, add water, yeast, and a little salt, and you've got dough. Dough! What an incredible invention. Depending on how you roll it, how you let it rise and rest, how you shape and then bake it, you can make

- a long, chewy baguette with a crispy crust;
- a circular, dense bagel;
- a flatbread called naan;
- and so many other bread products!

I knead gluten

At the very base of baking is a protein called **gluten**. This protein has been used so much by bakers over thousands of years that we could call it the incredible, edible gluten. The word comes from the Latin *gluten,* meaning "glue"–that's because it's sticky and elastic and binds everything together. Gluten is found in wheat and grains like barley and rye.

When you add water to wheat flour, the gluten becomes stretchy. You can feel this with your fingers when you knead dough. This repeated action develops the gluten in the flour and makes your dough elastic–it becomes almost as stretchy as bubble gum.

A molecular mesh

If you could see what was happening at the molecular level, you would realize that the gluten forms a matrix, or a mesh that holds everything together. The stronger the mesh, the chewier your bread will be. Sometimes you want to develop the gluten so your bread will be quite chewy–when you are making pizza dough, for instance. But other times, you want to handle the dough as little as possible; when you're making pie crust, less handling makes your pastry flaky and delicate. This is why cake and pastry flours are made out of different wheats with different amounts of gluten. Bread flour has more gluten than other flours.

I don't need gluten

Not everyone can eat gluten. In fact, gluten can make some people very sick. If you have celiac disease, you can never eat any gluten–not even a crumb. But that doesn't mean you can't eat delicious baked foods. More and more bakeries are offering cookies, cakes, breads, muffins, and doughnuts without gluten!

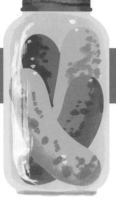

Preserve

Preserving food stops it from going bad. Preserved foods include pickles, jams, smoked fish, and so much more.

Why it started

At one time, people didn't have electricity to run fridges and freezers, so they had to find creative ways to make their food last. Throughout history, all sorts of delicious dishes were invented by people trying to make their food keep. Cheese preserved the milk that animals such as cows and sheep produced in large amounts in the summer. Dried meats (like pemmican and jerky) or cured meats (like bacon and prosciutto) were created to keep the flesh from rotting after an animal was killed. People also fermented fish and seafood to make sauces and pastes to flavor food.

Can it!

Canning fresh ingredients is practical, but also creative. The writer Sarah B. Hood knows why many people still want to make their own preserves. "If you live in a cold climate, you can't grow your own fruit and vegetables all year-round," she says. "It's really nice to be able to open a jar of fresh-smelling tomatoes or spread raspberry jam on your toast and remember what they looked like, and tasted like, in July. Making jam or pickles means using boiling water on the stove, so you have to be careful and pay attention to what you are doing. But it is easier than baking a cake. It is harder to make a mistake."

There are a number of methods used to preserve food

Curing To cure meat, you pack it in salt or put it in a salt solution. This draws out the water from the meat and preserves it.

Drying For thousands of years, people have used heat from the sun to dry their foods and make things like sun-dried tomatoes or pemmican.

Smoking When you smoke a food, you use a low-burning fire and smoke to kill the bacteria and dry out the meat.

Canning People figured out that if you heated food to a high temperature and sealed it shut in an airtight container, it could last a long time without rotting or making them sick.

Water

It's colorless. It's tasteless. And when it's flowing from the tap, it can be easy to take for granted. But water is precious to us—to life.

We drink water. We use water to cook and to clean. And without water, there wouldn't be food, because all plants and animals need water to grow. Farmers need to water their crops and their animals. In fact, humans use more water for farming than for any other activity. Everything we eat comes back to water!

Water your temperatures?
Water boils at 212°F (100°C) at sea level. When the atmospheric pressure changes—when you go up a mountain, for example—the temperature at which water will boil changes. No matter where you are, though, you need boiling water to cook foods and make drinks like tea.

Water freezes at 32°F (0°C). When it's this cold, we can make ice cubes and ice cream, and we can preserve our meats and veggies.

Water print
The amount of water it takes to make something is called its **water print**. This is a calculation of all the water used to grow and then prepare the food. It takes 10 gallons (38 liters) of water to make one slice of bread! So 10 gallons (38 liters) is bread's water print. If you think that sounds high, then imagine this:

it takes a mind-numbing 4,000 gallons (15 kiloliters) to produce just one hamburger!

Water in the kitchen
How many ways is water used in cooking? Let's see! We use water to

- boil foods like pasta and potatoes;
- steam foods like rice and veggies;
- turn bones into a rich stock to make soup;
- poach foods like eggs;
- sterilize canned foods such as jams and pickles.

What would we do without water?

In places on Earth where people don't have pipes that bring water into their homes, women and girls often spend a lot of their time walking from where they live to local wells and then carrying back water for the household. One study in Kenya found that many girls there carry heavy pots of water for more than 2 miles (3 kilometers) every day!

Chapter Four

What Is a Recipe?

A recipe is the list of instructions you follow to make a certain dish. A recipe will tell you what ingredients you need and how much of them. Most recipes tell you how many people the dish will feed and even how long it will take to make.

A recipe can be your key to learning how to make a new dish, so knowing how to use one is important. Some people think you don't need a recipe if you're a good cook, but this isn't true. Recipes help guide you in the kitchen. And cookbooks allow you to explore cuisines that may be unfamiliar or help you dream up flavor combinations you never would have thought of on your own. Even the greatest chefs will consult recipes—everybody can learn something new!

When you're learning to cook, it is helpful to read recipe books to get a feel for how different cooks handle the same ingredients. There are many cookbooks out there, so have a look and see what whets your appetite!

How to Read a Recipe

Recipes are a set of directions to help you make a dish in a certain way. Here are some guidelines for reading and using them.

Before you start

Read the entire recipe. Check to see that you have everything you'll need. Figure out how much time the recipe will take to make. Do you need to do anything before you start? Can you prepare what you want by dinnertime? Cooking a meal involves more than turning on the stove—you have to prepare your ingredients before you start putting them together, and this takes time. And some recipes have a surprise waiting at the end. You don't want to find out that you have to chill your custard for three hours if you want to serve it right away!

Yes, you have to do that!

Now you can start. Follow the instructions carefully. There are special words that the people who write recipes use to tell you what to do. A lot of these words—such as **sauté** and **dice** and **braise**—are explained in this book (see chapter 6). It's important to pay attention to these words if you want to make the dish as it was made by the author. If you stir-fry your meat rather than roast it, you aren't going to end up with the same dish!

Take note

Some people like to record their experiences cooking a certain recipe in the margins of the page after they're done. This technique can help you learn more quickly. If you found that a casserole needed more salt or a stew cooked more slowly than the recipe said it would, write that observation down. If you take note of what you've found, you'll know how to make the dish taste better the next time.

Proceed with caution

It's important to follow directions, but sometimes you have to make adjustments based on your circumstances. Every kitchen is different. That could mean medium heat on your stove is not quite the same temperature it was on the stove used by the person who wrote the recipe. So keep watch of what you're cooking. You don't want to ruin your stew because you were supposed to let it simmer for forty-five minutes, but it burned at thirty-seven. Also, choose a cookbook that suits your skill level. Sure, there are lots of fancy cookbooks out there, but when you're learning to cook, it's best to stick with a book for beginners.

What's in season?

Recipes are written by people who want to help you make good food. But they aren't usually written with the seasons in mind. If you pay attention to which ingredients are growing fresh in your area, you can make your food even more tasty! Find out which fruits and vegetables grow at certain times of the year and then try to incorporate them into what you are cooking. If you're making a pasta sauce in the spring, you might choose to add asparagus. But if it's August and zucchinis are ripe, you might use them instead. Just make sure that any ingredients you add to a recipe respect the character of the dish. You might not want to put early summer radishes in your macaroni and cheese rather than cauliflower—but then again, maybe you do. You never know what will taste good!

Did We Say Science? Actually, It's All Math

Have you covered ratios in math class? If not, a ratio expresses the relationship between two things as a number or an amount. If you were to put two olives and six mushrooms on your pizza, the ratio of olives to mushrooms would be 1:3. We often use ratios in baking and cooking (and less often for pizza math!).

Switching numbers

Changing the quantities of ingredients in a recipe will give you different results. For example, many of the ingredients listed in an oatmeal-raisin *cookie* recipe are the same as those listed in an oatmeal-raisin *muffin* recipe. But if you made both these recipes, you would end up with two quite different end products. What makes the cookie a cookie and the muffin a muffin is the ratio of sugar to flour to fat.

There are a few basic ratios you will need when baking. Ratios give structure to your experiments. They are made of parts. A part can be any measurement as long as it is the same type (such as a cup or a liter) for all ingredients. For example, to make cookies, you'll need:

- 1 part sugar
- 2 parts fat (such as butter, canola oil, or coconut oil)
- 3 parts flour

But for muffins, you'll need:

- 1 part sugar
- 1 part fat
- 2 parts flour

Plus to make the muffins, you'll need:

- 2 parts liquid (milk, for instance)
- 1 part eggs
- some baking powder

These are the key ingredients in their ratios. But if you change those ratios, you'll change the result—add a little more butter to the cookie recipe, and what you take out of the oven will be more chewy. If you cut the butter entirely, your batter won't stick together. If you mix only sugar and butter, you'll end up with icing instead.

This might sound complicated, but don't be scared away. When you want to make cookies, you don't have to figure out the ratios yourself. You can trust the recipe writer to do that for you. However, if you *understand* your ratios, you can figure out if the cookie is going to be chewy or crunchy based on how much of each ingredient the recipe calls for.

Ratios also apply when you're making other dishes. Such as when you are boiling bones to make stock. Or blending oil with egg yolk to make mayonnaise. Or when you are making a salad dressing. Once you know your ratios well, you can experiment as much as your taste buds can tolerate!

The incredible transforming dressing!

Salad dressing is one of the simplest and best ways to begin playing around within a recipe. To make a basic salad dressing, you'll need:

- 3 parts oil
- 1 part acid
- a little salt and pepper

There are so many different ways to make homemade salad dressing that you may never want to buy a bottle of the stuff again. First, choose an oil from the list at right. Then choose your acid and your flavor. Blend well. Dress your salad!

But don't be restricted by this list! You can experiment with whatever you find in your kitchen—just try to pick flavors that you think will go well together.

Oils

- Olive oil
- Nut oil, like walnut oil (as long as no one is allergic to nuts)
- Canola oil
- Grapeseed oil
- Avocado oil (this one's really expensive!)
- Sesame oil

Acids

- Apple cider vinegar
- Red wine vinegar
- White wine vinegar
- Balsamic vinegar
- Lemon or lime juice

Flavorings

- Maple syrup, honey, sugar, or agave syrup
- Mustard (avoid that bright-yellow hot dog mustard and look for something like Dijon)
- Fresh herbs like chives or tarragon (you can grow these yourself in pots)
- Garlic (roasted or fresh)
- Soy sauce
- Miso (fermented soybean paste)
- Fish sauce

Substitutions

Recipes can feel very bossy. They demand that you chop the zucchini into precisely sized cubes and then tell you to stir-fry it.

Of course, there's a reason for the demands—the recipe's writer wants you to taste exactly what he or she created. If you boil a chicken instead of roasting it in the oven as a recipe asks you to, you're going to end up with an entirely different dish. That would be a poached chicken—you wouldn't get the crispy skin of an oven-roasted bird that way!

What are substitutions, and how do they work in cooking?

But there's an exception to every rule. While it's important to respect your recipe, there are times when you don't need to listen to all the instructions. Just because the recipe calls for a particular ingredient, that doesn't mean you *have* to put it in. You have permission to ignore that bossy voice! After all, sometimes you may be missing one of the ingredients listed in a recipe. And other times, a dish will call for a flavoring you don't like. That doesn't necessarily mean you shouldn't make the dish.

Like for like

There is a catch, however. Until you are a very experienced cook, you should stick to substituting one ingredient for another that is most like it. That means you need to think of foods in categories. You can substitute, say, fleshy eggplant for similarly textured zucchini. Or thin green beans for asparagus. Pears for apples. Navy beans for lentils. Quinoa for rice. All of these things make great substitutions. But you can't replace eggs with yogurt. Or take out the flour and put in milk instead.

Is it in season?

What you put in a dish may also depend on the season. If you can't find good fresh plums, then you must either figure out what other fruit would work instead or wait to make the dish in the early fall, when plums are in full glory.

Does it match the cuisine?

The ingredient you want to substitute should also belong to the same flavor family as the rest of the dish. If you are making Mexican food, you probably won't want to add soy sauce. But then again, maybe one day you will be experienced and confident enough in the kitchen that you'll feel like adding soy sauce to your guacamole—and you'll never look back! The more you cook, the better you will become at making a recipe suit your tastes.

Don't be discouraged

Sometimes you change a recipe and the dish fails. Badly. That's okay! It happens to everyone. But try to learn from the experience. Think about why the dish didn't work. Then you can make it better the next time!

Do substitutions work in baking?

Short answer: **No.**

Long answer: **Sometimes, but you** *really* **need to know what you are doing. A cake, for example, will rise only if the batter contains the right balance of ingredients. A good rule of thumb with baking, especially if you're starting out, is to follow the recipe precisely.**

How to Measure

Let's say you want to make a dozen muffins. The recipe is probably going to ask you to measure out the following ingredients:

- 2 cups (500 mL) of flour
- 1 tbsp. (15 mL) of baking powder
- ½ cup (125 mL) of oil (and a few other ingredients)

It's important to measure the ingredients correctly and put only the right amount in your bowl—especially when you are baking. Here's how to do it.

To measure flour

Fill your measuring cup right up to the line that marks the amount the recipe calls for. Make sure the surface of your flour is flat and level. Take a look at it from the side of the cup to get a good view. If you put in too much flour, scrape off the extra by dragging the flat back of a knife across the edge of the cup.

In some parts of the world, people weigh their flour on a kitchen scale instead of putting it in a measuring cup. It's a different way of doing things, but the scale tends to be more accurate. So if you are using a European recipe in particular, you'll need a kitchen scale. If you don't have one, stick with North American recipes for your baking.

To use a measuring spoon

If you are measuring something like baking powder, you will want to scoop it up in a measuring spoon. Run the flat back of a knife blade over the top to level the powder, and push off any that's poking up.

If you're measuring a liquid like oil or vanilla extract, pour it directly into a measuring spoon—but do this over a plate or the sink, not your mixing bowl. If you pour too much of your liquid into the spoon and it overflows, the plate will catch the spill. This ensures you don't end up adding too much to your recipe. You also might be able to save the spill and use it for something else later.

To measure a liquid

You measure a liquid such as milk or lemon juice the same way you would a dry ingredient. You can use a measuring cup or a measuring spoon, depending on how much the recipe calls for. European recipes usually measure liquids in milliliters. Don't worry—you'll find these marked on most measuring cups, too. (And if not, just use the conversion chart at the back of this book!)

How do you measure a cup of butter?

It's not easy to press slightly softened butter into a measuring cup. A trick to measuring butter is to use cold water. If the recipe calls for half a cup (125 mL) of butter, start by putting half a cup (125 mL) of water in a glass measuring cup. Then add chunks of butter until the water reaches the 1 cup (250 mL) mark. That's two times the half. (If you need 1 cup [250 mL] of butter, you'll start with 1 cup [250 mL] of water and make the level rise to 2 cups [500 mL].) If the water level rises too much, take some butter away. If the water level is not high enough, then add a little more butter. At the end, scoop out your butter and pour away the water.

The Many Ways to Cook a Carrot

When you think of vegetables, you probably don't think of dessert. And fruits aren't usually used in the main course. Or are they? Ingredients can be incredibly flexible. Recipes can show you how!

Bananas for dinner!

People use the ingredients they have available to them in all sorts of unexpected and delicious ways. Bananas can be combined with ground beef to make a coconut curry. Avocados can be used to make savory soups and zesty guacamole, or they can be blended with sugar and milk to make sweet puddings, milkshakes, and even popsicles. Many savory dishes are made with dried fruits. Though sweet potatoes are often eaten with a main course, they also can be coated with candied sugar and served for dessert.

With a little creativity, we can turn any ingredient into just about any kind of dish!

The incredible, edible carrot

Which brings us to the carrot. The incredible, edible carrot. Carrots can be eaten raw, cooked, baked, or boiled. There's carrot soup, carrot soufflé, carrot juice, carrot salad, carrot casserole, and carrot curry.

Then there are all the sweet things carrots can make: cakes, puddings, and a fudge-like treat called halwa. In fact, you could base a whole meal around this orange root vegetable. And though not every ingredient is as flexible as the carrot, here are three recipes to show how one vegetable can be the star of some very different dishes.

Carrot Salad

Makes 6 servings

- 1 lb. (450 g) carrots
- 1 lemon
- 2 tbsp. (30 mL) olive oil
- 1 tsp. (5 mL) ground cumin
- salt to taste
- optional: raisins or dried cranberries

1 Peel the carrots. Grate them with your cheese grater. Put the grated carrots in a bowl.

2 Squeeze the lemon into another small bowl. Mix with the olive oil and cumin. Add a good pinch of salt.

3 Dress the salad, mixing in the dressing well. Add a handful of raisins or dried cranberries—if you like them.

Carrot Muffins

Makes 12 muffins

- 2 cups (500 mL) all-purpose flour
- ½ cup (125 mL) sugar
- 1 tbsp. (15 mL) baking powder
- ¼ tsp. (1 mL) salt
- ½ cup (125 mL) melted butter, plus a little soft butter for greasing
- 1 large egg
- 1 cup (250 mL) milk
- 1 cup (250 mL) grated carrot
- 2 tsp. (10 mL) cinnamon
- optional: ⅓ cup (80 mL) raisins

1 Preheat oven to 375°F (190°C) degrees. Grease a 12-cup muffin tray with the soft butter.

2 Mix together the flour, sugar, baking powder, and salt in a large bowl.

3 Mix together the melted butter, egg, milk, grated carrot, and raisins (if using) in a medium bowl.

4 Using a dry spoon, make a well (or valley) in the center of the dry ingredients. Pour the wet ingredients into the well. Mix until just combined (see Q & A on page 79).

5 Fill the muffin cups evenly with batter.

6 Bake for 20 minutes, or until a knife stuck into a muffin comes out clean.

Carrot Soup

Makes 6–8 servings

- 2 lb. (900 g) carrots
- 1 large onion
- 2 tbsp. (30 mL) olive oil
- 1 tsp. (5 mL) ground cumin
- 1 in. (2.5 cm) fresh ginger
- 5 cups (1.25 L) water
- salt to taste
- lemon, cut in half to squeeze
- optional: ¼ cup (60 mL) coconut milk

1 Peel the carrots and onions, and chop them into small pieces. Chop or grate the ginger.

2 Heat the olive oil in a large saucepan on medium heat and add the onions. Cook them, stirring often, until they are light brown—about 5 minutes.

3 Add the cumin and the ginger and cook for one minute. Then add the chopped carrot, stirring.

4 After a couple minutes, add the 5 cups (1.25 L) of water and the salt and bring the pot to a boil.

5 Turn down the heat and simmer for 20 minutes, or until the carrot is soft.

6 Let the soup cool a bit. Puree the soup with a blender, hand blender, or masher until smooth. Add salt and a squeeze or three of lemon juice to suit your taste buds. If you are adding coconut milk, stir it in now.

Chapter Five
Getting Ready in the Kitchen

You don't need a lot of stuff to cook good food. Some chefs even say that all you need to make a nice meal is one pot and a knife.

Home cooking is all about turning what you have into something delicious to eat. It can be like the old folktale *Stone Soup*, which is about a stranger who arrives at a village and turns a pot of boiling water and a stone into a delicious meal by tricking villagers into adding different ingredients.

That said, if you want to cook meals quickly and easily, you'll need a clean, well-organized kitchen stocked with some basic ingredients. Keeping clean and staying organized will help your kitchen run smoothly. It's really hard to make rice if you don't know where your rice is kept! And if you don't have any rice in the cupboard, you aren't going to be able to whip up a pot of it for your dinner. But then again, if you *only* have rice in the cupboard—no pasta, no other grains, no potatoes—then your diet might lack the variety you need to be healthy.

So let's get organized and oriented in the kitchen. This chapter will also help you to think about how to plan your meals so that they're healthy, fun to make, and tasty to eat!

The Tools for the Job

TV chefs sure make cooking look easy. But that sparkly clean kitchen filled with gadgets and gear is really a set—it's only built to look perfect on television.

Your home kitchen doesn't need all those fancy gizmos, or even new cupboards and granite countertops. If all you have are the things listed below, you'll do fine. And if your parents don't have some of this stuff, don't spend a lot of money to get set up. Instead, head over to your local thrift shop. Choose things that are in good shape (watch for chips, rust, and cracks), and with a scrub they'll be as good as new! Remember that when it comes to cooking utensils, you should choose wood and metal over plastic.

Tools you need to prepare your ingredients

Wooden cutting board

Sharp knife A paring knife is a good place to start for small hands, but you can work your way up to a chef's knife if your parents think it's okay.

Vegetable peeler
to peel vegetables like potatoes and carrots (with parents' okay)

Whisk to whip up cream and egg whites or blend a pudding or sauce so it doesn't have lumps

Rubber or silicone spatula
to scrape your bowl so you don't waste any batter when you are baking foods like muffins and cookies

Measuring cups
to measure your dry and wet ingredients

Measuring spoons
for measuring smaller ingredients like baking powder and vanilla extract

Grater
to grate cheese and vegetables like beets and carrots

Cooking utensils

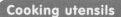

Tongs to pick up hot foods without burning your fingers

Spatula to flip pancakes and omelets

Point-sensitive meat thermometer

Ladle for serving soups, stews, and sauces

A few wooden spoons for stirring of all sorts

To help with the cooking

Colander large enough to drain pasta

Soup pot

Frying pan

Saucepans at least two, one small, one large

Baking sheets for cookies, fries, veggies, and more

Lasagna pan for making brownies as well as casseroles

For after you're done cooking

Glass containers with lids for your leftovers

Dishcloths to wipe down your countertops

Soap and scrubber for doing the dishes

Tea towels for drying those dishes (be sure to launder them regularly)

FOOD FACT: Slip grip

When using a cutting board, try placing a damp towel or rubber mat underneath it. This prevents the board from slipping and makes it safer to use.

Stocking Your Pantry

If you're going to start to cook, it's good to have some basics on hand. This will save a trip to the store every time you want to eat. By keeping a few handy basics in your cupboards and your freezer, you will always be able to whip up a meal in a pinch. Here are some starter ingredients.

Oils You can get away with using two oils for everything you do in the kitchen. Olive oil for dressings and lower-heat cooking, and canola oil for high-heat cooking. But it's useful to have other oils, too, including grapeseed oil and sesame seed oil. Make sure you store all your oils in a cool, dark place.

Beans and other legumes Chickpeas, lentils, black beans, red beans, lima beans—legumes like these are your ticket to a quick dinner. When they come pre-cooked in a can, they can be used to make a meal in a flash. And you can keep dried legumes in old glass jars for soups and stews.

Flours Whole wheat and unbleached white flour are great for baking. If you can't eat gluten, stock up on gluten-free flours, such as those made from sorghum, millet, and rice. You will also need baking soda and baking powder.

Sugars Recipes will often call for white or brown sugar, and sometimes both. You can also use unrefined sugars, such as honey or maple syrup.

Pasta It's nice to have an assortment of pasta shapes to choose from. You could stock your cupboard with a long pasta, like spaghetti or fettuccine, and a couple of shaped pastas, such as penne or rotini. Whole wheat pasta is more nutritious, so opt for that whenever possible.

Rice and grains There are so many kinds of rice—jasmine, sticky, basmati, red, black, and more. Keep several varieties in your pantry. Other grains, such as millet, work well, too. Also try quinoa (technically a seed but cooks like a grain) or couscous (tasty little grain-like balls made from wheat).

Canned tomatoes Use canned tomatoes to make soup, fresh salsa, sauce—they are possibly the best canned good to have on hand. Some people also recommend keeping a jar of pre-made pasta sauce in the cupboard, but they're loaded with sugar. Instead, make an easy sauce with a can of tomatoes, some olive oil, a bit of basil, and whatever else you want—there's a recipe at the back of the book. (And make sure you read about BPA in cans on the next page, too.)

Nuts and seeds Nuts and seeds are not only good for you but can add some zip to your breakfast when sprinkled over fruit and yogurt. They're also tasty with lunch (try pumpkin seeds on a salad). And dinner (add nuts to a stir-fry). Seed or nut butter even makes a quick snack if you spread it on bread or crackers.

Spices and herbs Spices and herbs will define your cuisine. If you like to cook Italian or French food, stock up on dried basil, oregano, rosemary, and parsley. Indian cooking calls for spices like cumin, coriander seed, and turmeric. Asian foods are likely to incorporate ginger. Note that almost every cuisine uses garlic and onions, so always have some of those on hand.

Fresh ingredients You can't always have the same foods in your fridge because things come and go with the seasons. Still, you should always try to keep some cheese, fresh fruits, and vegetables. But pay attention to what you have in those produce drawers—you don't want to have to throw out food! Potatoes and root vegetables, such as carrots and beets, keep a long time and are a good pantry staple.

Frozen ingredients Frozen peas just might be the best convenience food. You can add them to soups, stews, and salads. You can even snack on them (instead of chips), by the handful, frozen—try it! Bread and tortillas are freezer-friendly, too.

BPA—no thanks!

When buying canned goods—especially tomatoes—you should look for ones that are marked "BPA-free." BPA is the abbreviation for bisphenol A. That's a chemical used to make all sorts of things, including the lining of tin cans. BPA is not good for the human body, even in small amounts.

"BPA screws up hormones and is linked to some pretty nasty diseases," says Rick Smith, who wrote a book titled *Slow Death by Rubber Duck* about chemicals that are bad for you. "The good news is that it's avoidable. The main source of BPA in our daily lives is the interior lining of some cans. We're talking everything from pop to soup. So eat fresh or frozen food whenever you can and look for 'no-BPA' labels when you buy canned food. 'Cause who really wants a dollop of BPA in their spaghetti?"

Condiments add zing to your food

Some are spicy, some are sweet. Some you use when you're cooking, others you add directly to the food on your plate, with a squirt. Ketchup, anyone?

- soy sauce
- mustard
- chili sauce
- ketchup
- honey
- maple syrup
- fish sauce
- vinegar

Going Grocery Shopping

Being in charge of your home's grocery shopping will give you a taste of adulthood. Sure, you could buy ice cream and sugary cereal, but if you want to cook real food, you'll have to buy the ingredients you need—and make sure you don't spend more than your budget.

Start by making a list

What do you need to make your meal? If your recipe calls for only part of a cauliflower, think about another dish you can make the next day with the remaining pieces. Do you need any ingredients for *that* dish? Plan ahead! Also think about what fresh fruits and vegetables are in season.

Make a budget

You can find olive oil that costs fifty dollars a bottle. Or you can buy some for eight dollars. So what can you afford? How much money do you have to spend? How can you use that money best?

Tricks to saving money:
- Look at what's on sale.
- Buy bigger packages of food— sometimes the big bag of flour costs less per unit than the little one.

(But not always. Calculate how much you are paying per 100 grams. In big supermarkets, this information is often posted in small numbers on the price display.)
- Check out the section full of fruits and vegetables that have been marked down to sell quickly. (Just use them fast, before they go bad!)
- Buy dry legumes, such as chickpeas or black beans. These cost less than the ones that come in a can.
- Look for your grocery store's own brand of products and see if they are less expensive. Brand names tend to cost more.

Things to avoid to save money:
- Kits of all kinds, such as a cupcake-making kit that comes with cake mix, icing mix, and sprinkles. These prices are marked up.
- Foods you probably won't eat. You know those free samples in supermarkets? They are there to try to get you to buy that product. But if you don't normally eat that food, you probably won't eat what you've just tried when you get home.
- Buying a food just because it's on sale. You won't save money if you don't eat it!

What's a farmers' market?

A farmers' market is a place where farmers come together to sell their food. Over the past ten years in North America, farmers' markets have become very popular, and today you can find them in many towns and cities. Usually, the farmer herself is selling you the food. So if you buy a head of lettuce for two dollars, the farmer gets to keep that money. When you buy lettuce at the supermarket for the same price, the store keeps its share of the profit, and this means the farmer earns less overall. The average farmer makes only about ten cents out of every dollar spent at the supermarket! That's why lots of family farms prefer to sell their food at the farmers' market.

And there's another advantage to these markets: they make it easier to tell which vegetables are in season, and therefore fresher and tastier. At the supermarket you can find just about anything, at any time of the year.

EXPERT ADVICE:
Taste! Smell! See! Try!

"Taste things! Take a chance," says cookbook author Naomi Duguid. Naomi has traveled to countries such as China, Vietnam, and India to research her award-winning cookbooks. To do her research, she hangs around village markets, watching people work with food. She spends time at hawker stalls that serve street food to observe the sellers preparing their dishes. She visits people in their homes, learning to cook from them so she can share their recipes in her books. When she travels, she eats new foods every day.

Naomi encourages all of us to adopt a little of her zeal for experimenting. And good news: you don't have to travel to the other side of the planet to try new flavors! She suggests becoming a food tourist in your own city or town by buying something different at the supermarket or the local ethnic grocery store. Or poke around the farmers' market, and when you see something you don't recognize, buy it! "Why not taste all the ingredients and find out and explore?" Naomi says.

Diet and Health

People can talk a lot about what they eat and why. And when they do, they often talk about diets. There are all sorts of diets.

There's a vegetarian or vegan diet. There's a lactose-free or sugar-free or gluten-free diet. There's the no-carb diet, the no-yeast diet, the raw-food diet, and many more. People follow some diets to lose weight and others to address specific health issues—sometimes both. But there is one diet we all should follow: a healthy diet. It's not so much a diet as a way of buying, cooking, and eating good food that will nourish your body and keep you growing strong.

What is a healthy diet?

A healthy diet features lots of plant-based foods, such as fruits and vegetables, as well as legumes, such as chickpeas and lentils.

A healthy diet is full of variety. To help get this variety and to ensure you get all your nutrients, some people suggest eating a "rainbow" of colors. There are lots of options to make this rainbow. You could try:

- sweet peppers for red
- carrots for orange
- lemons for yellow
- broccoli for green
- blueberries for blue
- grapes for purple

The more colors of the rainbow you can get on your plate, the better. And when you're looking at that plate, try to ensure that half of the foods in front of you are fruits and vegetables.

The pros of protein and more

You also need the protein that you get from meat, nuts, legumes, and fish. Protein plays a key role in important body functions like making hormones and repairing damaged tissues. And don't forget about carbohydrates, which give your body energy, or the many other things that come from your food, like fatty acids and amino acids.

If you cut out a certain food—if you're a vegetarian, for instance, and don't eat meat—you have to make sure that you are still getting the nutrients and proteins you need. That's why vegetarians choose high-protein foods such as legumes (chickpeas, lentils, and black beans) and tofu.

Good food choices

There are simple choices you can make to eat a healthy diet.

- Skip the soda and juice, and choose water instead.
- Grab an apple or some carrot sticks instead of a bag of chips or a candy bar for an after-school snack.
- Challenge yourself to make a fresh dip like salsa or guacamole to go with your chips. Those tomatoes and avocados are full of nutrients—not that you'll notice!

Above all, it's easier to have a healthy diet if you cook from scratch. If you cook for yourself, you will know what ingredients you're putting in your body. This way, you can be sure your body is getting what it needs to be healthy. So eat well and stay active! That's the best diet of all.

Not-so-fast, fast food!

A typical fast food meal of a hamburger, fries, and a soda has a bad rep these days—for good reason. While it might be a tasty meal, it's filled with all sorts of things that are bad for your body, including highly processed ingredients, as well as lots of sugar and fat. More and more people agree that we should be eating foods that come from plants and not as much meat. It's okay to have that burger once in a while as a treat, but it shouldn't be a regular meal.

Ethics in the Kitchen

Adults often say that you should never talk about religion or politics at a dinner party. It turns out, though, that food is all about religion and politics. People's cultural and religious beliefs shape what they eat, and their political attitudes sometimes guide them, too.

Here are just some examples of the way religion shapes what people eat.

- Observant Muslim and Jewish people do not eat pork.
- Some Catholics don't eat meat on Fridays.
- Many Hindus and Buddhists are vegetarians.

Are there any food rules in your family that have their roots in religion?

Get political

A lot of people also think about the way their food affects other people, animals, and the planet as a whole. What you choose to buy has an impact on the world. This is why some people adhere to food principles that reflect their politics and their point of view.

What's a vegetarian?

A vegetarian is usually someone who doesn't eat the flesh of another living being—although some vegetarians do eat fish and other seafood. A person could make the decision to become a vegetarian because he or she doesn't like the way that animals like cows and chickens are treated in our food system. Someone else may choose to go vegetarian because it is better for the environment. The worldwide meat industry is a major source of the greenhouse gases that cause climate change.

What's a vegan?

A vegan is someone who doesn't eat any food that comes from an animal. So vegans not only avoid all meat, fish, and seafood, but also won't eat butter or milk or cheese or eggs. They have to find other ways to get important nutrients.

What's up with all the labels?

A lot of people want to know how the food they buy was grown or produced. Labels help the consumer to tell one product from another, but that doesn't mean that they're not a little confusing.

Here's a short guide to help you along.

Organic You can buy organic eggs, milk, meat, fruits, and vegetables—and even organic processed foods. If a food is marked "organic," that means it meets a bunch of criteria set out by the government. Organic foods are grown without chemical pesticides or fertilizers. In the case of animals, the word "organic" means they are fed organic foods and don't receive antibiotics unless they are sick. Organic food products tend to be more expensive.

Cage-free These are eggs from birds that aren't kept in cages. On many large farms, hens are stacked in cages, one on top of the other, with little or no room to move (these are called battery cages). Many people find this to be cruel. There is now a movement in North America to get more farmers to produce cage-free eggs.

Free-range These are eggs from birds that live in a barn with space to move around and access to the outdoors—it doesn't mean the birds are just living outside in the fields. Eggs from these birds tend to be from very small farms and you buy their eggs at the farmers' market. Free-run eggs are from hens that have space to perch and move but no access to the outdoors.

Fair-trade This term is used to describe the practice of ensuring that farmers in typically poor countries are paid fairly for their food. So if a farmer in a developing country sells his sugar or chocolate under a fair-trade agreement, he should be treated well and paid a decent price. Fair-trade rules also usually encourage farmers to take care of their environment. You might notice a fair-trade label on your chocolate. This means that the cocoa beans used to make the chocolate were not picked by children, who are forced to work instead of going to school and treated poorly.

Sustainable fisheries Humans are harming the oceans by catching so many fish that schools can't produce enough babies to keep their numbers steady. Fish that is certified as "sustainable" has been caught more responsibly—that is, without overfishing or damaging the ocean floor with equipment.

What is food security?

People have food security when they are always able to eat enough healthy food to fill their stomachs and nourish their bodies. There is enough food grown on Earth to feed all of us well. The problem is that lots of children and adults go hungry every day, in both poor countries and rich countries. When people talk about food security, they mean that they want to make sure every person on Earth can eat the food he or she needs to stay healthy.

FOOD FACT: Skip it!

If you want to help the planet, eat less meat! You don't have to become a vegetarian to reduce your **footprint**. Even if you get your family to skip eating meat one day a week, you will make a difference.

Chapter Six
How to Make That Meal

So now it's time to cook. This is going to be good, because cooking can be lots of fun. We make a big deal about eating home-cooked food with family and friends on special occasions, but we don't need to reserve this kind of effort for those few days of the year. Cooking good food and sharing it with people we care about feels great just about any day.

When cooking, it's important to be prepared and to take things slowly at first. Plan out what you're going to do, and think ahead. Be careful and patient. There are all sorts of techniques you can use to prepare your meals. Your role as cook is to figure out which ones best suit what you are going to make.

After all, what kind of meal do *you* want to make? Are you preparing brunch for Mother's Day or a meal for another special holiday? Is it your turn to make dinner for the family after school? Make sure that what you prepare matches the occasion. A simple dinner is perfect for a weekday meal. On the weekend, you may be able to spend time cooking something more challenging. And you might want to go *all out* for a holiday meal.

Then, when your food is ready, set the table and call your dinner mates to join you. You'll all have the chance to enjoy some home-cooked food—together.

Get Prepped!

A recipe will ask you to do all sorts of things to your raw ingredients before you start cooking. These steps are called the prep—short for "preparation."

The way you prepare your ingredients will affect your final dish. For example, we cut food in different ways because their shapes and sizes affect the way they cook—and the way they taste. Once you become comfortable with these different techniques, you can mix it up a bit—by replacing a dice with a slice, let's say—and change a recipe to suit your own tastes.

First step: Knife skills

To slice or dice, you will need knife skills. In other words, you'll need to learn how to use a knife safely. If a knife can cut a carrot, it can cut your finger pretty badly, too. So practice first with something easy. (Remember to ask an adult before using a knife.) Try chopping mushrooms with a butter knife. Then move up to a zucchini and a steak knife. Once you get the hang of chopping, ask an adult if it's okay for you to use a sharper knife.

Basic knife safety

- Always cut away from yourself.

- Make sure your fingers aren't in the way before you cut.

- If you drop your knife, let it fall—don't try to catch it!

- Always pass a knife to someone else handle first—don't point a knife at anyone.

- Don't run with a knife in your hand.

- Use a knife only for cutting—a knife isn't a hammer or a can opener.

The way to prep

Here are some of the methods cooks use to prepare their raw ingredients.

Peel When you peel a carrot or a potato, you use a vegetable peeler to remove its rough outer layer, or skin. A recipe may ask you to peel apples, pears, zucchinis, and more. You don't need a peeler to peel an onion or a garlic clove, however. Instead, you simply cut the top and tail off with a knife and use your fingers to peel the papery outer skin.

Chop Many recipes start by asking you to chop onions. This means taking a knife and cutting an onion into many little pieces. Sometimes a recipe will ask you to chop **finely.** That means you should ensure that your pieces are extra small. A **rough chop** is when it doesn't matter what the final product looks like. You only need to get that onion chopped. It doesn't have to be pretty.

Slice If you slice something, you are cutting it into flat pieces. You can be asked to slice something thinly or thickly.

Dice To dice a vegetable—like a carrot, for example—is to cut it into small cubes.

Mince A mince is a very, very fine dice. Meat is often minced— in Great Britain, people call ground beef "minced meat."

Grate Learning to grate cheese is one of the best ways to start your cooking career. All you need is a thingy called a grater. This is a flat piece of metal with a rough surface. Rub your cheese (or your carrots, or your beets) on this rough surface to make tiny little pieces. But beware of grating your knuckles!

Zest To zest an orange is to shred the outer skin with a fine grater. You can zest a lemon or a lime, too. Best to use organic fruit that has been grown without chemical pesticides—and wash them very well before grating.

Mash Bet you know this one. You take an ingredient and crush it using a tool called a masher or a fork. Usually a recipe will ask you to mash a vegetable after you've cooked it. But not always— mashed raw bananas are an important ingredient in banana bread.

FOOD FACT: The chop

The word "chop" can also mean a certain cut of meat. Pork and lamb are the most common kinds of chops.

FOOD FACT: Getting fancy

Of course, chefs know all sorts of fancy ways of cutting food. They make a **chiffonade** by rolling leafy greens into cigar shapes and slicing them into thin strips. They can **julienne** potatoes and zucchinis and other firm vegetables by cutting them into matchsticks. They can even make a super-small dice called a **brunoise**.

FOOD FACT: Fruit fixin's

You can do a lot of different things to fruit to get it ready for a dish. Take an orange. You can zest it. You can segment it (break it into pieces) or you can juice it. Apples can be peeled or chopped or quartered—or even grated. Bananas are usually sliced or mashed.

Cook It!

An incredible thing happens when you put raw ingredients over a fire. Tomatoes become sauce. Bones and water become broth. A piece of cow becomes a roast. Imagine what the first person to put a piece of raw food on a stick and hold it over fire thought when she took a bite. Yum!

Food likes it hot

Today you're more likely to cook with a stove than an open fire. (Though many people around the world cook over an open flame because they don't own a stove.) There's a lot more to cooking than simply putting your raw ingredients over the heat. The way you cook will shape *what* you're making. It will make the difference between, say, a pot roast and a stew. Or a stir-fry and a steak. Or a soup and a sauce. If you cook over intense heat, your dish will be very different from one that is simmered slowly over low heat. And a dish cooked on the stove won't taste quite the same as one you cook in the oven.

There are the various ways you can cook your food. And lots to consider. How hot should it be? How long should you cook? How should the heat be applied to the food? Here's a guide to what to think about.

On the stovetop...

The stovetop is the everyday cooking tool for most people. Some stoves have electric elements for cooking, while others have gas burners. Here are some common stovetop cooking techniques.

Boil When you boil something, you submerge it in water that is so hot, bubbles appear in the pot. A **rolling boil** is when the water in your pot is churning almost violently. Turn down the heat and you'll end up with a **simmer**. This is a slow, bubbling boil that will cook your soup or your stew delicately.

Fry When you fry a food, you cook it in a shallow pan, using only a little bit of fat. This is very different from deep frying. When you **deep-fry** something—like a doughnut, a French fry, or a pakora, you submerge it in boiling oil. A **stir-fry**, on the other hand, is when you quickly fry small pieces of vegetables, meats, or tofu over high heat. The trick to not burning your dinner is to constantly stir the food in the pan.

Caramelize When you caramelize something, you cook it slowly for a long time, until all its natural sugars turn to caramel.

Sauté To sauté something means to fry it quickly in hot oil or butter. This word comes from the French for "to jump." A really experienced chef might make her vegetables jump in the pan by tossing them a bit, but you don't have to do this if you don't want to!

Brown You brown something when you cook it over high heat for a short period of time until it turns brown. You might brown carrots, celery, and onions before you add them to stock to make soup. You could also brown meat, such as beef.

Steam To steam a vegetable, you boil water and use the resulting steam to cook. This is a gentle cooking method because you don't submerge the food in the water.

FOOD FACT: Put a lid on it!

Put a lid on your pot when you boil water. Not only will the water come to a boil faster, but you will save energy, too.

In the oven...

When you use a stove, you cook on top of your heat source. When you put food in the oven, you surround your food with hot air to cook it.

Some ovens are called **convection ovens**. These have a fan that moves the air around the food. This ensures that all areas of the food receive the same amount of heat. The oven is the kitchen appliance that uses the most energy—and convection ovens use the most of any ovens! So try to make good use of your heat by cooking several things when you turn your oven on—don't just bake a few potatoes!

Of course, there's a lot you can do in your oven besides bake.

Broil If that turkey you're roasting isn't browning on top, you can broil it. This is when you expose your food to very high temperatures. Most ovens have a broil setting that cranks up the heat in the top part of the oven. Beware: This cooks food very quickly—which means it also burns easily! You need to keep a close eye on things that are broiling.

Roast Roasting surrounds food in the dry heat of an oven or a fire—only at a hotter temperature than baking. We roast meats like chicken, turkey, and beef. You can also roast vegetables. (Roasted squash or potatoes are heavenly.) Most dishes are roasted in metal or ceramic pans. Never put anything with plastic handles in an oven—they'll melt.

Oven and stovetop together

A few cooking techniques make use of both the stove and the oven.

Pan roasting This technique combines **searing** (this makes food crisp on the outside) with roasting. First, the meat is seared on a very hot stovetop. Then the dish is moved to a hot oven to roast for several hours.

Braise To braise meat, you start by browning your ingredients on high heat on the stovetop. Then you add some liquid, turn down the heat, and cover your dish with a lid. You'll need to leave it to cook for several hours, either inside your oven or on the stovetop. Because the dish cooks for so long, the meat and the vegetables become incredibly tender.

On the barbecue...

The barbecue is an outdoor cooking device that burns either gas or charcoal to create heat.

Food is cooked over an open flame on metal bars called a **grill**. Although you can close the lid and use your barbecue a bit like an oven, grilling is the thing a barbecue does best.

Grill We grill food directly over a heat source, without the help of a pan. If you like sausage from the barbecue, you like your sausage grilled. Those black lines you can see on your food are called **grill marks**.

In the microwave...

A microwave cooks food by shooting it with—you guessed it—microwaves!

These are similar to light waves and are invisible to the eye. When microwaves shoot through food, they make the water molecules inside the food vibrate. This heats it up! Microwaves are very handy for warming up leftovers, melting butter and chocolate, and heating milk. In the 1980s, it became popular to cook all sorts of foods in the microwave, but meat tends to taste better cooked on the stovetop or in the oven.

Caution: Never turn on an empty microwave! It could break. Also, never put metal in the microwave; it will reflect the waves back into the machine and damage it—or even start a fire. Finally, be careful when removing dishes from the microwave, as they can be very hot.

The solar oven

Usually, the heat we cook with comes from gas or electricity. But there's one huge source of heat that we don't often think of using to cook our food: the sun! To harness this energy, people build **solar ovens**. These are airtight boxes that capture the sun's rays so the heat cooks the food inside. A good solar cooker has shiny reflectors to help direct more sun into the oven. The heat can reach temperatures that are high enough to cook fish or bake a cake—though the process does take longer than in a traditional oven.

Choose Your Own-ion Adventure!

You know by now that the way you handle a certain ingredient determines how it turns out. Play this game to see how this works. Take one onion and choose its fate!

START HERE:

One onion, sliced. The raw onion is firm and crisp, like an apple. *How does it taste?* Sharp and strong. And when you cut it, it might make your eyes water.

Stir-fry

Add other veggies, such as red peppers, eggplant, and beans, to your fried onions. Stir your ingredients quickly over a hot flame and you have a stir-fry.

Fry

Cook the onion at high heat in a pan, with oil or butter. What do you get? Fried onions! *How does it taste?* The onion slices have softened, and the sharp flavor has softened, too—it might have only a little zing.

Caramelize

Cook the onion at low heat so its sugars brown and turn to caramel. What do you get? Caramelized onions! *How does it taste?* The onion slices are now soft and slippery. They taste sweet, and the sharp onion flavor has disappeared.

Pizza

Caramelized onions are great on pizza.

Boil

Cook the onion in boiling water or stock. What do you get? Soup! *How does it taste?* The onion is now soft and translucent. If you fish out a piece to eat on its own, it will taste a bit watery. The sharp onion flavor is gone.

Vegetable soup

If you boil your onion in a pot of chicken stock with some chopped vegetables—potatoes, carrots, celery, cabbage— it will help build the flavor of the soup. You may not be able to taste the onion on its own anymore, but it will have boosted the flavor of your dish overall.

Char

Cook the onion over high heat until slightly burned and a little blackened. What do you get? Grilled onions! *How does it taste?* The onions haven't cooked through and still have some of their original color. They might even crunch a bit in your mouth. The sharp onion taste is still there, although its volume has been turned down a bit.

Shish kebab

If you spear the onion on a skewer—along with other vegetables and maybe some pieces of chicken—then cook it on a grill or a barbecue until a little charred (not too much or it'll burn), you'll end up with a shish kebab.

Baking Is Magical

The way you combine and handle ingredients when you bake will determine whether your croissant is flaky, your bread is chewy, or your bagel is dense. Baking draws on the characteristics of different ingredients.

- **Butter** and other **fats** help make our baking soft.
- **Eggs** help ingredients stick together.
- **Egg whites**, when beaten into a stiff foam, make our baking light and airy.
- **Sugar** ensures that our baked goods are sweet; it also makes them brown.
- **Yeast**, **baking soda**, and **baking powder** all release gas to help our dough and batter rise.

Time to bake...

Cookies, brownies, muffins, pies, cakes, scones, and more! There are so many yummy foods to bake. But although a pie is different from a brownie and a cookie is nothing like a scone, many of the same techniques are used to make all these delicious treats.

Creaming Recipes for some cakes and most cookies will tell you to cream the butter and the sugar. To do this, your butter must be soft enough that you can sink your finger into it. Unless it's really cold in your house and the middle of the winter, all you need to do to soften your butter is let it come to room temperature. Then, using either a whisk or a wooden spoon (you could also use an electric mixer), beat the butter until it is a lighter yellow color. Then slowly add the sugar until it is thoroughly mixed in.

Folding When you're asked to fold in your ingredients, it means to carefully combine them. You may be asked, for instance, to gently fold your egg whites or whipped cream into a heavier batter made up of your wet and dry ingredients—this is so you don't burst the tiny air bubbles that make up your foam. Use a spoon or rubber spatula to slowly cut your batter down the middle and then lift it up and fold it over, into the center of the bowl. Work your way around until you've folded it all in.

Separating eggs Often a baking recipe will ask you to separate the egg yolk from the white. You do this to make custards, meringues, angel food cake, and other desserts. It's a good idea to clean the egg first by rinsing it under running water and then carefully drying it. Work over one bowl and have a second bowl nearby. Crack the egg gently near its middle and pull open the shell, making sure to catch the yolk in one half of the shell. Let the excess egg white drop into the bowl below. Pass the yolk gently back and forth between the two shell halves until all the white falls into the bowl. Now that you've separated the egg, put the yolk in the other bowl.

Whipping You might also be asked to whip cream or eggs. You do this by beating air into the liquid until it becomes foamy. The longer you beat it, the stiffer the foam becomes. When a recipe says to beat egg whites until stiff, you want to be able to form them into a pointy mountain peak.

Baking Q & A

Why do you first mix wet and dry ingredients separately?
You mix your dry ingredients together before combining them with the mixed wet ingredients to help you blend all the elements of your recipe. This helps ensure that ingredients like baking powder are mixed in evenly.

What's the difference between baking powder and baking soda?
The difference between these two white powders is minor—baking powder is baking soda plus some acid salts. Like yeast, both baking powder and baking soda produce carbon dioxide bubbles that make dough rise.

What does it mean when a recipe says "mix until just combined"?
A recipe for a quick bread or a muffin will often warn you not to overwork your batter by mixing it too much. "Mix until just combined" means you should use some restraint when you're mixing your dry ingredients with your wet ingredients. Mix the two together using the fewest strokes possible.

What's a cake mix?
A box of cake mix will save you a few steps when you bake a cake. Inside you'll find a dry mixture that already includes the flour, baking powder, sugar, and flavoring. The instructions on the box will tell you to add an egg, some water or milk, and a fat (usually an oil). These mixes have been engineered by food companies to work pretty much every time.

Food Safety

Cooking is fun, but it's not foolproof. If you're not careful, you can hurt yourself or even make other people sick. The risks are small, however, as long as you take some precautions to stay safe and healthy in the kitchen.

Here are some basic rules to follow.

- **Check with an adult to make sure it's all right to cook,** especially if you plan to use the stove, a knife, or an electrical appliance.

- **Wash your hands** with warm water and soap before you begin. Lather for as long as it takes to hum the alphabet. If you touch raw meat or eggs when you're cooking, wash your hands again—right away.

- **Wash your ingredients** before you use them. Take special care to thoroughly wash the vegetables you will eat raw in a salad (even if the package says something is prewashed!).

- **Use different cutting boards for meats and vegetables.** Try cutting meat on an old plate that you can clean in the dishwasher.

- **Always cut away from yourself,** never toward yourself.

- **Avoid baggy sleeves** that can catch on the burner of the stove and potentially start a fire.

- **Treat your raw meat very carefully.** Throw away packaging immediately—and if you have a dog or a cat, make sure your pet can't get to the bloody wrappers. Clean up any drips and spills of blood as soon as they happen, and then wash your cloth well. Wash your hands each time you touch raw meat. Don't use a utensil for uncooked meat and then use it again for something else without washing it in between.

- **Keep cooked food separate from raw ingredients**—especially raw meat. Also, never place cooked meat back on the same plate that held it when it was raw.

- **Wipe up any spills** before you slip on them!

- **Tie your hair back** when you're cooking. This will keep your hair out of your food and away from hot burners on the stove.

- **Turn off the stove when you're finished.** Don't place anything on top of a hot burner, especially your skin.

Those nasty bugs

We're not the only creatures who like our human food. Bacteria, viruses, and molds all like to make their home in our food, and these guys can make us really sick. When you get sick from something you eat, this is called **food poisoning**. To avoid this, wash your hands, keep your work surfaces clean, and make sure you keep the food at the right temperature. Bacteria multiply at between 40°F (4°C) and 140°F (60°C). That means leftover food must be cooled first and then refrigerated—but don't leave cooked food sitting on the counter for longer than two hours. Most leftovers don't keep for longer than three days in the fridge either, so label everything carefully. Keep a roll of masking tape and a marker in the kitchen to note the date when you put the food away.

You don't want any E. coli 0157 in your hamburger

E. coli 0157 is a particularly nasty bug that can make you very sick. One place *E. coli* hangs around is in raw hamburger meat. That's in part because ground beef is usually made from the odds and ends of many cows, and so it's more likely to

Wash those hands!

Raw meat can carry all sorts of bad germs, including some that are resistant to antibiotics. So skip the disinfecting spray and use good hygiene instead.

be contaminated. The good news about *E. coli* is that you can kill it with heat. That's why it's so important to cook all ground beef until it is done right through—you don't want any pink on the inside. But looks aren't always accurate. Food safety experts suggest that you buy a point-sensitive meat thermometer to ensure that you cook your ground beef to 160°F (71°C) every single time.

Melon head!

The folks who study food safety suggest that when you buy a cantaloupe, you should wash it before you cut into it. Cantaloupes have a thick, rough skin that microbes like to cling to. You can get rid of them with a scouring pad and some water and even a squirt of soap! And it's not only melons that need a scrub. It's a good idea to wash all your fruits and vegetables thoroughly.

Fast Food, Homestyle!

It's fun to create a beautiful meal in the kitchen, but you must eat at least three times a day, and that means sometimes you have to move fast. If you practice a little bit, it's possible to make healthy homemade dinners more quickly than you can get a takeout hamburger.

The trick is knowing how to work with your pantry staples, a few fresh ingredients, and maybe even some leftovers you happen to have in your fridge.

Here's how you can get a healthy meal up and running using nothing more than two pots and a little time.

Pot #1:
Choose your base

- Is your meal going to be a rice bowl?
- Or a pasta bowl?
- Maybe you have another staple you can cook, like quinoa?

Whatever you pick, put some salted water in Pot #1, get it on the stove, and cook your base.

Pot #2:
Choose your protein and veg

- Do you have any leftover cooked meat in the fridge, like roast chicken or some steak? How about a can of black beans or chickpeas?
- And how about a vegetable? Will it be frozen peas or fresh, rinsed spinach? (You don't even have to chop it—watch it wilt, or shrink down, with the heat!)

Put Pot #2 over medium heat with a little oil. Start with your protein, then add your veg about 5 minutes later. Stir often until everything is cooked through, around 10 minutes total.

 Pot #2 (Again!):
Choose your toppings

Now add your flavor toppings to Pot #2. Ask yourself which toppings go best with whatever is already in the pot. You could try:

- Soy sauce
- Olive oil with some fresh herbs
- Seeds or nuts
- Grated cheese
- Sour cream or yogurt
- Chili sauce
- Or anything else that you think will taste good

Time to eat!

As they say, don't sweat the small stuff. Make whatever you have chosen work for you. And if your meal isn't your greatest creation ever, who cares? At least you filled your stomach with healthy food—and saved money by not going out to eat.

On the other hand, if you really liked what you did, try to remember which ingredients you used. With a little more time and planning, you could make that dish taste even better the next time. It might become a new favorite!

Eggs, eggs, glorious eggs!

Eggs are the greatest fast food ever. You can turn them into just about anything. How about scrambled eggs for dinner? Or maybe a fried egg sandwich? An omelet? Even use them to make pancakes. To make it feel like dinner, grate some cheese on top, fry up some mushrooms, steam broccoli or cauliflower, and dig in!

Set the Table. It's Time to Eat!

After you've made such an effort to prepare a meal, do it justice by serving it at a nicely set table. In different parts of the world, setting the table means different things. Here are four common ways to set a table.

The Western table:

On the western table, the fork goes on the left and the knife on the right. The spoon is placed on the outside of the knife, while the glass sits on the placemat above the knife. If you're eating more than one course, you'll add a smaller salad fork to the left of the dinner fork. Now you're ready to invite the Queen of England over.

- A butter knife belongs on the side plate.
- The dessert fork and spoon sit horizontally above the plate.

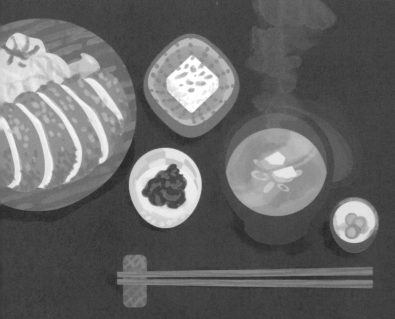

The Japanese table:

For a formal Japanese meal, close attention is paid to the way the food looks and how it is presented. Food is often served in small dishes (a rice bowl, a soup bowl, and so on), rather than on one dinner plate, as is common in the West. Each little dish should be no more than two-thirds full, so the person eating can appreciate the pattern on the ceramic.

- Chopsticks are always placed at the bottom of the setting, pointing horizontally.
- The rice sits on the left.

The Ethiopian table:

Before you eat an Ethiopian meal, it is a custom for someone to pour water over your hands at the table. After your hands are cleaned, the food is served. At the centre of an Ethiopian meal is the flatbread injera that is often made from a grain called teff.

- The injera serves as a kind of plate—your food is dished right on top of it.
- You tear the injera with your right hand (never your left hand) and scoop up saucy dishes. No utensils are used for eating.
- After the meal, it is tradition for someone to pour water over your hands once again.

The Indian thali:

A thali is a type of plate used throughout India. It also refers to a way of dining, where meals are served on a stainless-steel platter. Each thali holds rice and a flatbread as well as a number of small dishes, each in their own little container. These dishes could include salad, some curries, and even a sweet called a table dessert to liven your meal.

- You eat from the thali using your right hand, not utensils.
- A little bowl of water with a lemon slice can be offered to wash your hands.

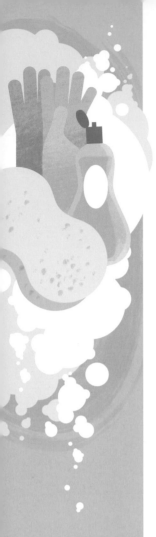

Cleaning Up

You've created your masterpiece and enjoyed the results of all your hard work. But don't forget the cleanup! A big part of cooking is tidying up after you're through. The people you live with will be happier to have you cook if you don't leave a mess behind. (Although you can always ask them to help you!)

Here are some basics to cleaning up.

- **Throw out the trimmings as you go.** Don't let those onion skins, potato peelings, and carrot tops lie around. Toss them out as you cook.

- **Do the dishes.** Clean all the dishes, pots, and utensils you used to make your meal.

- **Wipe down your workspace.** Use a clean cloth to wipe the kitchen counters, the table, or wherever you prepped the meal. You don't need to use an antibiotic spray to clean your kitchen. A clean, damp cloth is usually good enough. If you want to get more DIY, mix equal parts of white vinegar and water and keep that in a spray bottle for cleaning.

- **Sweep or vacuum the floors.** No need to track crumbs around your house.

- **Put away the clean dishes once they've dried.** There. That looks much better!

Food waste

It's hard to believe but more than 30 percent of the food grown in North America is never eaten. It ends up in the garbage instead. When we throw food out, we're not only missing out on all that nutritious stuff, we're also wasting the water that went into growing the food and the energy it took to process and transport it. And if you tossed your own leftovers, you would also be wasting all the effort you made to cook the meal in the first place! The good news is that there are some simple steps to avoid wasting food.

1 Don't buy more than you need.

2 Look inside your fridge and see what ingredients you can turn into a meal, rather than creating a meal based on a recipe (see 92–93 for hints on how).

3 Enjoy your leftovers.

4 You can freeze most leftovers you can't finish right away—label the container with the date and contents. Then when you're wondering what to make for dinner one night, you can pull out a ready-made meal! Soups, stews, and cooked meats freeze very well if they are packaged to keep the air out.

What happens if you don't like what you've made?

Good question. This is practically guaranteed to happen, especially if you're experimenting with new recipes. Here are some strategies for those inevitable mistakes.

1 Waste not, want not! Pretend you are a super-mature adult at a dinner party and eat it anyway. Who says we have to love every meal, right?

2 As the saying goes, one man's meat is another man's poison. Or in this case, one kid's poison is another person's meal. Offer the dish to a friend or family member. Maybe that person will love it!

3 Think of some creative ways to turn the meal into something different. What if you add some ketchup? Can you mask the taste with something else you like, such as hot sauce?

4 Make something else the next time.

Keepin' it clean

Luis Valenzuela grew up in the town of Toluca, Mexico, playing soccer, going to school—and never venturing into the kitchen. But when he was fifteen years old, he announced to his parents that he wanted to cook food for a living. "My mom said, 'Why do you want to be a chef? You've never cooked anything!'" he remembers. "I said, 'Mom, I've never done surgery on anyone either. I've never done *anything*!'"

Today, Luis runs a busy restaurant kitchen, and he knows just how important it is to make sure it's kept clean and organized. "Having clutter, it clutters the mind," he says. When the restaurant kitchen is clean, his staff can focus on making delicious food for his customers.

Even if you don't have plans to become a chef, Luis has three reasons to keep your own kitchen clean. "One, if it gets dirty, little animals and insects will come in and have a snack," he says. "Two, you want to have it clean so you can invite your friends over lunch. And three, if your kitchen is clean you can mess it up again!"

Conclusion
So What Dish Will You Make?

Welcome to the end of this book! Already, you've covered so much ground. You've learned about how your senses work to help you taste your food. And about how we use science in the kitchen every day. How to prepare and cook your food. And how to set the table.

And even if you haven't ventured into the kitchen yet, you now know how to cook. Yes, you do! Just by reading this book, you'll have enough information to get started. The only thing left to do is practice.

So where to start? Decide what you want to make. Maybe you'll follow your gut and go with your creative instincts. Check out what's in the fridge or the cupboard, and go.

But you don't need to venture too far on your own right away. To help you out, I've put together a list of cookbooks with easy recipes for kids and beginner cooks. (You can find the list at the back of the book.) Choose a simple recipe— but also one for a dish that you'd love to eat—and then pick a day to start cooking. Make sure you give yourself lots of time to make mistakes, to fumble, and then to create your masterpiece. (Don't worry if it doesn't taste—or look—like a masterpiece.) Assemble all the ingredients and equipment you need. And then dive in!

Cooking is important. It's a skill you can take with you anywhere. As you get older, it will become even more important to know how to cook. And no matter what you cook, remember that whenever you mix together raw ingredients to make food, you are feeding your stomach, your heart, and your soul. And hey, it's fun, too.

There are thousands of recipes to make, but here are four that you may find yourself using again and again because they are simple and good to eat!

Quick and Simple Pasta Sauce

Makes 4 servings

- 1 small onion
- 1 garlic clove
- 1 28 oz. (796 mL) can whole or diced tomatoes, or 1 lb. (450 g) fresh tomatoes
- 2 tbsp. (30 mL) olive oil
- salt and pepper to taste

1 Finely chop the onion and garlic. If you are using fresh tomatoes, cut off the stems and remove the hard white core. Cut tomatoes into small pieces.

2 Heat the olive oil in a medium saucepan. Add the onions and garlic to the pan. Cook, stirring occasionally, until lightly browned—about 5 minutes.

3 Add tomatoes to the pan. Sprinkle with salt. Lower the heat to a simmer and cook for about 20 minutes, until mixture has thickened. Your sauce will look a bit chunky. For a smoother sauce, simmer on very low heat for about an hour.

Note: Eat this basic sauce as is or jazz it up with fresh or dried herbs such as basil or oregano. For a bolder sauce, try adding chopped olives, slivers of anchovy, or dried chili flakes.

Yummy Lentil Soup

Makes 6–8 servings

- 1 cup (250 mL) dried red lentils
- 1 medium onion
- 1 garlic clove, chopped
- 2 stalks celery
- 2 carrots
- 2 medium potatoes
- 2 tbsp. (30 mL) olive oil
- 6 cups (1.5 L) water, or chicken or vegetable stock
- 2 bay leaves
- salt and pepper to taste

1 Pour lentils onto a plate and pick out any tiny stones. Put lentils in a strainer and rinse them in cold water.

2 Peel onion, garlic, carrots, and potatoes. Chop onion, then garlic, celery, carrots, and potatoes.

3 Heat the oil in a large saucepan on medium heat. Add the onion, stirring until brown—about 5 minutes. Add the garlic and stir for about a minute before adding the celery, carrots, and potatoes.

4 Add the water or stock and the bay leaves. Add the lentils and stir. Then bring to a boil.

5 Lower the heat to a simmer and cook for about 30 minutes, until lentils are tender. Add salt and pepper to taste.

Never-Buy-Cereal-Again Granola

Makes about 12 servings

For the base:

- 6 cups (1.5 L) large flake oats (not instant)
- ¾ cup (175 mL) honey or maple syrup
- oil for greasing the pan

1 Preheat oven to 350°F (180°C) degrees.

2 Lightly grease a large baking tray or pan.

3 Warm the honey or maple syrup in a small saucepan over low heat. Remove from heat when the sweetener is runny.

4 Spread the oats in the tray and pour the honey or maple syrup over the oats, stirring to mix in well.

5 Bake the oats for 15 minutes, then take the tray out of the oven to stir the mixture. Bake for 15–20 minutes longer, until lightly browned. Keep a close watch to make sure the oats do not burn.

Add these extras to personalize your granola:

- 1 to 2 cups (250 to 500 mL) unsalted nuts or seeds. If you like, toast these by adding them to the granola tray during the last 5 minutes of baking.
- ½ cup (125 mL) dried, unsweetened coconut
- 1 cup (250 mL) raisins or other dried fruit, like apricots, dates, or figs

Store granola in a container with a tight-fitting lid. It keeps for about two months.

Outside-the-Box Oatmeal Cookies

Makes about 24 cookies

- 8 tbsp. (125 mL or 1 stick) unsalted butter, softened at room temperature
- 1 cup (250 mL) brown sugar, packed
- 2 eggs
- 1 tsp. (5 mL) vanilla extract
- 1 ½ cup (355 mL) all-purpose flour
- 1 ½ cup (355 mL) large flake oats
- 1 ½ tsp. (7 mL) baking powder
- ¼ tsp. (1 mL) salt
- a little butter or oil for greasing sheets
- optional: ½ cup (125 mL) chocolate chips or raisins
- optional: 1 tbsp. (15 mL) ground flax seed

1 Preheat oven to 375°F (190°C). Lightly grease two cookie sheets with butter.

2 In a large bowl, use a wooden spoon to mix the softened butter with the sugar until combined. Add the eggs and stir to combine. Add the vanilla and stir.

3 In another bowl, combine the flour, oats, baking powder, and salt (and flax seeds, if using). Then slowly add these dry ingredients to the butter mixture. Stir until no patches of dry flour remain. Mix in the chocolate chips or raisins, if using them.

4 To form each cookie, spoon a heaping tablespoon of the dough onto the cookie sheet. Leave two inches between cookies so that they can spread out while baking.

5 Bake for 10–12 minutes, or until the edges of the cookies start to brown lightly. Remove from sheet to cool on a wire rack.

What Goes with What?
A Guide to Flavor Pairings

When you are starting to improvise in the kitchen, it can be a good idea to draw on long-loved combinations of flavors. Here's a quick list of foods and spices that go particularly well together.

1 Italian

Herbs like
- basil
- bay leaf
- oregano
- parsley
- rosemary
- sage
- tarragon

Go well with fats like
- butter
- olive oil

And acids like
- lemon juice
- vinegar (red wine, white wine, or balsamic)

And veggies like
- celery
- garlic
- mushrooms
- onions
- potatoes
- red peppers
- tomatoes

And foods like
- hard, sharp cheeses, such as Cheddar and Parmesan
- legumes (chickpeas, cranberry beans, navy beans, or fava beans)
- meats (chicken, lamb, beef, or pork) and fish

2 Asian

Flavors like
- garlic
- ginger
- green onions
- leeks

Go well with herbs and spices like
- black pepper
- cilantro
- cloves
- sesame seeds
- star anise

And sauces like
- hot sauce
- miso
- rice vinegar
- soy sauce

And fats like
- peanut oil
- sesame oil
- sunflower oil

And veggies like
- bok choy
- broccoli
- cauliflower
- edamame (fresh or frozen soybeans)
- green beans
- mushrooms

And proteins like
- cashews
- legumes (adzuki beans or chickpeas)
- meats (chicken, beef, or pork)
- peanuts
- tofu (firm)

3 Indian

Herbs and spices like
- cilantro
- cinnamon
- coriander seed
- cumin
- fennel seed
- fenugreek
- ginger
- mustard seed
- saffron
- turmeric

Go well with flavors like
- coconut milk
- garlic
- hot chilies
- onions
- tomatoes

And acids like
- lemon juice
- lime juice

And fats like
- ghee (clarified butter used in Indian cooking)
- grapeseed oil
- sunflower oil

And proteins like
- legumes (chickpeas, lentils, or mung beans)
- meat (chicken or beef) and white fish
- paneer (an unripened cheese used in South Asian dishes)
- yogurt

4 Mexican

Flavors like
- garlic
- onions
- red and green peppers
- tomatoes

Go well with herbs and spices like
- basil
- chilies
- cilantro
- cumin

And acids like
- lemon juice
- lime juice

And fats like
- canola oil
- olive oil

And proteins like
- legumes (black beans, kidney beans, or navy beans)
- meat (pork, chicken, or beef)
- sharp, hard cheeses, such as Cheddar
- soft, creamy cheeses, such as feta or queso fresco
- sour cream

Measurements and Conversions

How do you know if your meat is cooked? How many grams make up 4 ounces? And what do I set the Fahrenheit gauge on my oven to if the recipe calls for 180°C? (The answer is 350°, by the way.)

These kinds of questions come up all the time—so here are some answers!

Cooked meat temperatures

The color of your meat doesn't tell you whether it is done. To be safe, use a point-sensitive meat thermometer to check the temperature of your meat before serving. Here are the ideal internal temperatures for different types and cuts of meat.

- Beef, veal, and lamb
  (pieces and whole cuts)
  medium-rare 145°F (63°C)
- Beef, veal, and lamb
  (pieces and whole cuts)
  medium 160°F (71°C)
- Beef, veal, and lamb
  (pieces and whole cuts)
  well-done 170°F (77°C)
- Pork (pieces and whole cuts)
  160°F (71°C)
- Poultry, such as chicken, turkey,
  or duck (pieces) 165°F (74°C)
- Poultry (whole) 185°F (85°C)
- Ground meat of beef, veal, lamb, and pork
  (e.g., burgers, sausages, meatloaf, casseroles)
  160°F (71°C)
- Ground meat of poultry 165°F (74°C)
- Egg dishes 165°F (74°C)

Dry volume conversions

Imperial	Metric
⅛ tsp.	0.5 mL
¼ tsp.	1 mL
½ tsp.	2 mL
¾ tsp.	4 mL
1 tsp.	5 mL
1 tbsp.	15 mL
¼ cup	50 mL
⅓ cup	75 mL
½ cup	125 mL
⅔ cup	150 mL
¾ cup	175 mL
1 cup	250 mL
2 cups or 1 pint	500 mL
3 cups	750 mL
4 cups or 1 quart	1 L
½ gallon	2 L
1 gallon	4 L

Weight conversions

Imperial	Metric
½ oz.	15 g
1 oz.	30 g
3 oz.	85 g
3.75 oz.	100 g
4 oz.	115 g
8 oz.	225 g
12 oz.	340 g
16 oz. or 1 lb.	450 g
2.2 lb.	1000 g or 1 kg

Liquid volume conversions

Imperial	U.S. fluid oz.	Metric
2 tbsp.	1 fl. oz.	30 mL
¼ cup	2 fl. oz.	60 mL
½ cup	4 fl. oz.	125 mL
1 cup	8 fl. oz.	250 mL
1 ½ cups	12 fl. oz.	375 mL
2 cups or 1 pint	16 fl. oz.	500 mL
4 cups or 1 quart	32 fl. oz.	1000 mL or 1 L
1 gallon	128 fl. oz.	4 L

Oven temperature conversions

Fahrenheit	Celsius	Gas mark	Heat description
225	110	—	very cool/very slow
250	130	—	—
275	140	1	cool
300	150	2	—
325	170	3	very moderate
350	180	4	moderate
375	190	5	—
400	200	6	moderately hot
425	220	7	hot
450	230	8	—
475	240	9	very hot

A note on the internet...

You can find all sorts of recipes on the internet for, well, pretty much *any* food. Just remember that a lot of mistakes can also find their way onto the internet, so check the comments section on a recipe you want to try before proceeding—often errors will be mentioned.

Further reading

There is no shortage of cookbooks out there, but for first-time cooks, some are better than others. These excellent books are written simply and clearly and work well for the amateur chef.

How to Cook Everything and *How to Cook Everything Vegetarian* by Mark Bittman (Wiley, 2008/2007)
If you're going to have only one cookbook in your kitchen, this one is it. *How to Cook Everything* has all the basic recipes you'll ever need—and many more advanced ones to try as your skills improve.

Jamie's Food Revolution by Jamie Oliver (Hyperion, 2011)
This book is a perfect guide to everything from fun snacks and breakfasts to full-sized family dinners. It also includes loads of info on kitchen basics, such as how to stock your cupboards and how to add exciting flavors to your food.

Fast Flavours: 110 Simple, Speedy Recipes by Chef Michael Smith (Penguin, 2012)
This excellent collection of recipes is designed to keep things quick and easy.

The New Enchanted Broccoli Forest and *The New Moosewood Cookbook* by Mollie Katzen (Ten Speed Press, 2000)
These classic vegetarian cookbooks are a great introduction to cooking and feature a huge variety of simple but delicious recipes.

Index

Concepts
Bacteria 23, 36, 41, 80, 81
BPA 17, 61
Cage-free 67
Diet 64–65
Energy 7, 10, 64
Fair-trade 67
Food safety 70, 75, 80–81
Food security 67
Free-range 67
Gelatin 35
Gluten-free 40, 64
Healthy eating 64–65
Organic 67
Processed foods 16–17
Proteins 34, 64
Science 33–43
Sustainable foods 67
Temperature 12, 34, 35, 81, 92
Vegan 64, 67
Vegetarian 64, 67

Culture and history
Expert advice 17, 19, 57, 61, 63, 87
Farmers' market 63
Fusion 27
History of food 22–23, 24, 25, 26, 27
Migration of food 23, 26–27, 30, 31
Politics 31, 43, 66–67
Regional cuisines 21–31, 84–85
African 25, 85
Asian 21, 25, 61, 84
French 21, 22, 25, 26, 61
Indian 21, 25, 61, 85
Italian 21, 22, 26, 61
Mexican 22, 24
North American 21, 24, 27, 84
Religious diets 66
Supermarket 16, 31, 62–63
Table settings 84–85
Transportation of food 30–31
Weather and climate 18, 22, 23
Work, influence on food 28–29

Foods and ingredients
Beans 50, 60, 92, 93
Bread 40, 41, 78
Butter 38, 48, 53, 78, 92, 93
Canned goods 42, 60, 61
Carbohydrates 10, 64
Carrots 54–55
Cheese 9, 14, 18, 19, 41, 42, 83, 92, 93
Chicken 18, 24–25
Chocolate 8, 14, 19, 67
Cookies 48, 78, 91
Dough 40, 41, 78
Eggs 33, 39, 67, 78, 79, 83, 91
Fats 10, 38, 48, 78, 79, 83, 91
Fish 29, 39, 64, 67
Flour 38, 40, 41, 48, 52, 60
Fruits 10, 15, 19, 30, 61, 62, 64, 67
Fungi 41
Gluten 40, 64
Grains 10, 60, 82, 91
Grocery shopping 60–63
Herbs 49, 61, 83, 92, 93
Leftovers 75, 82, 86
Legumes 50, 60, 62, 64, 82, 90
Lemon juice 8, 39, 93
Meats 10, 18, 24–25, 29, 30, 34, 36, 64, 67, 73, 74, 80, 82, 92, 93
Nuts 61, 64, 83, 92
Oils 18, 38, 49, 60, 83, 91, 92, 93
Onions 13, 70, 76–77, 92, 93
Pasta 22, 60, 82
Rice 11, 21, 22, 25, 60, 82
Salt 8, 10, 36
Soup 24, 60, 77, 90
Spices 23, 61, 92, 93
Stocking pantry 57, 60–61
Sugar 8, 34, 37, 48, 60, 73, 78
Tomatoes 26, 60, 90, 92, 93
Vegetables 10, 18, 25, 29, 30, 34, 50, 54, 55, 61, 62, 63, 64, 65, 66, 67, 73, 74, 76, 82, 92, 93
Vinegar 8, 39, 49, 92, 93
Water 36, 41, 43

Recipes
Adjustments to recipes 47, 49, 50, 51, 54, 76, 82
Carrot muffins 55
Carrot salad 54
Carrot soup 55
Conversions 94–95
Cookbooks 23, 45, 95
Cookies 91
Dressing 49

Flavor pairings, guide to 92–93
Granola 91
Lentil soup 90
Measure, how to 52–53
Measurements 94–95
Pasta sauce 90
Quick meal ideas 82–83, 92–93
Ratios 48–49
Read recipes, how to 46–47, 79
Seasonal ingredients 24, 28, 30, 47, 51, 63
Substitutions 50–51

Taste and flavor
Aftertaste 9
Artificial flavors 16–17
Bitter 8, 11, 14
Changing tastes 14, 15
Mouth 10, 12
Natural flavors 16, 17
Salty 8, 14
Senses and taste 12–13
Smell 12, 13, 17, 18
Sour 8, 39
Spicy 9, 11, 23
Supertasters 11
Sweet 8, 14
Taste, general 7–19
Taste, how to 19
Taste buds 10–11, 14
Tastes, five 8–9
Terroir 18
Tongue 10–11
Umami 9

Techniques and tools
Baking 38, 40, 48, 51, 52, 53, 60, 78–79
Barbecue 75
Boiling 43, 73, 77
Braising 74
Brining 36
Broiling 43, 74
Browning 73
Canning 42
Caramelizing 73, 77
Chopping 70, 71
Cleaning up 80, 86–87
Cooking techniques 72–77, 82–83
Cookware 59
Creaming 78
Curing 36, 42
Dicing 71
Drying 42
Folding 78
Freezing 35
Frying 24, 38, 73, 76
Grating 71
Grilling 25, 75, 77
Kitchen utensils 58–59
Kneading 40
Knife skills 70–71, 80
Marinating 39
Mashing 71
Microwave 75
Mincing 71
Oven 29, 74, 75, 95
Pan-roasting 74
Pasteurization 16, 34
Peeling 70
Poaching 43
Preparing ingredients 70–71
Preserving 16, 36, 37, 39, 42
Proofing 41
Roasting 24, 74
Sautéing 73
Slicing 71
Smoking 42
Steaming 73
Stovetop 73, 74
Whipping 79
Zesting 71

Editorial consultants

June Jo Lee Co-owner, Readers to Eaters; Vice President, The Hartman Group
Martin Kouprie Chef & Co-owner, Pangaea, Toronto, Canada